Words to
Ease Your Soul

Words to
Ease Your Soul

Messages to guide the spiritual path

JACQUI ROGERS

Author of the Best-Selling *Simply Spiritual*

ISBN 978-1-907203-93-0

Typesetting by Wordzworth Ltd
www.wordzworth.com

Cover design by Titanium Design Ltd
www.titaniumdesign.co.uk

Printed by Lightning Source UK
www.lightningsource.com

Cover images by *http://creativecommons.org*
and by Sylvie Gotti, with thanks

Clip Art by Art Explosion, with thanks

Published by Local Legend
www.local-legend.co.uk

**LOCAL
LEGEND**

For Ray, whose support inspires me to keep writing.
Also for Melanie: I may wear the armour but she has the sword,
and we shall succeed because we believe.

Acknowledgements

This book is written with gratitude to Arthur,
with thanks for his words and for his love and wisdom;
also to Fah Hian for his strength and to Dave.
These are three of my spirit helpers who guide me daily.

Previous Publications

Simply Spiritual (ISBN 978-1-907203-69-5)
Published by Local Legend in paperback and as an eBook.

This Book

Words are so important. They can stir us into action and lift us from despair. But we don't all have someone to offer those words to us when we need them, though we all deserve to hear them.

This book is inspired by spirit for when you need that little extra help. Here, the spirit world speaks to you as it speaks to me, so please read these passages as if they were written just for you and let their power show you the way forward. I believe that within each passage is a hug sent from the spirit world directly to you!

The writing is for when you are searching for the words to change your life, to inspire you and to make a difference for yourself and for others, to open up to amazing possibilities and to know how special you are. May your beautiful soul be eased.

The writing is grouped into themes. But you may choose to allow the power of your higher mind to guide you to the passage that you need right now. Hold the closed book in both hands and meditate a while on the issues that concern you, then open it at random...

With love,
Jacqui Rogers

Jacqui's website is *www.simplyspiritual.org.uk*

Contents

The Journey of Life   1

Our Relationships   45

For Times of Sadness   93

Spirit Guidance   123

THE
JOURNEY
OF LIFE

Journey

The sun spreads across the western sky,
the hues of red and puce shine brightly like an artist's colours
that someone has let loose.
I stand beneath this vision here, now wide open on the plains,
as shadows flash upon the ground,
a mess of scattered stains.

But I know this sight so very well,
I see it daily as I walk this Earth;
I see it by night and I have seen it from my birth,
Wakan Tanka's display of strength and love
to show what power exists.
And we marvel and create the legends from such views by
        sunlight kissed.

Mother Earth provides us with all we need
to live in this, her lovely place.
But it grows smaller every day as our needs encroach the space.
Is it need? Or is it greed? We must decide between the two
for it's our choice that in the end will make the best of me and you.

This Earth will bring you all you need in life,
so say the stories long ago,
the legends that we pass down from the sacred buffalo.
We thank our great-grandfather for all the life he brings,
we thank the strongest eagle
for the shelter of his wings.

The sacred pipe of buffalo gives the cleansing smoke
to purify a vision quest for everyone to signify
a gain in greater knowledge that is linked to the greater goal –
expanding who we are, growing within our souls.

So will we listen to the words? I ask because so many have not
    done,
Nor taken responsibility, yet blaming everyone.
We have to know ourselves right now,
as our ancestors look down from above,
so that we may do what they could not –
    find peace and brotherly love.

Responsibility

The candle burns solitary and alone, the only light in the room and the only source of comfort for the inhabitants. There they sit, condemned by their fellow man for something that they did not do, resigned to their fate, resigned to know that truth does not really matter and all that seems to be is what deems to fit the situation. There is a great sadness and a defeat for the loss of so much to come and what has been; their punishment is the ultimate, their life.

How can we imagine the feelings of one who is condemned to die? Being maligned at the hand of another when their cause has been just? Can we only empathise or sympathise with the case, with the people or with the cause? Or do we wipe responsibility from ourselves? Are we going to judge the same as everyone else? Or are we going to sing our own songs and follow what is in our hearts? Throughout all ages and all cultures this has been happening. We hear the lament "Protect the innocent" but if only this were always the case – perception is the key, and it is important to find the one that fits correctly. Are we going to judge?

It is very difficult not to do this. We all do it every day of our lives. Is it an opinion or a judgement? What's the difference? And do we use the same information to come to that decision? Interesting isn't it? How many times has someone judged you because the situation fits, and you must be the wrong-doer – when you know that you are totally innocent? Who listens when you cannot prove that fact? As in the case of so many before, the answer is "Very few" – unless they have discovered who they are and have the moral strength to overcome their peers.

We may not be condemned to lose our life, but we may be condemned on another level. People believe what they hear.

Indeed, when they hear it they have a choice to acknowledge the truth or not of the opinion or judgement raised. So we must all decide if we want to pass it on. But beware that sometimes idle gossip can be misconstrued as fact… My opinion may not affect me if it is about someone else, but what if it were said about me – how would I feel? How would I feel to be maligned incorrectly? We must not justify loose words and feelings, for we have not walked the path of that other person and we do not know what they have endured to get to this place in time.

We all need to be aware and responsible for who we are, what we say and what we do. No longer can we pass blame onto another and escape the consequences. We will all face what we do on this plane of life when we get to the next! Be aware that no-one judges us outside of our Earthly plane – only we will do that ourselves, so be mindful of that fact.

We all have so many opportunities to advance and move onward, so that when we arrive in the spirit world we arrive at the correct place we need to be for our onward journey. We cannot be perfect, that is impossible or we would not be here. But on the paths we tread we can attempt to be a little circumspect, see the reality, see the facts and not the hype. The truth is always there, we cannot say it is hidden; we cannot say "We did not know" because we do. We have been shown by all the ages and the people who have gone before just how bad things can be, how much the following of even one person can bring to our world in one way or another.

I hear you say "I already do this" – but the people I know don't. And that is a judgement in itself. I am sure that they are saying the same thing about me. So what can we do about them? Not a lot really, is the truth. All we can do is live our lives by example, being leaders to show the way of love and respect, showing that we can talk the talk and walk the walk because we know it is the right thing to do. Some of us have been conditioned by the past, by our heritage; but we have a choice, there is always a choice to follow or to lead. They cannot judge you because you choose a different way, as that is your pathway not theirs.

So let us be responsible for our lives, for all we do and who we affect. Let's send the love, the help when needed, and protect the innocent and show the correct way to be – and there is always room for improvement. We all know what this is and we must know it is possible. If we all did this, do you think there would be a difference? We know the answer to this, if only we all chose it.

So choose it and find your path, and it will always be bathed in light.

Don't Give Up

Life is difficult,
every day a challenge.
Every day some more stress
loaded on your already overborne shoulders.
How do you cope?
Can you cope?
Of course you can!
Your love is special, always protected,
so stop giving away your power.
Keep it for yourself,
be a little selfish right now.
It will serve your soul.
And when you are fixed
your love can flow again.

Listen

When you want that change so much...
When you want to move forward in your life...
When you have given all you can
and still to no avail
and the frustration can't be tamed...
Stop.
Just cease.
To do nothing it is to do all.
Silence can be very deafening.
And sometimes we just have to wait.
Our dreams and gifts will be of greater service
when we relinquish control
and sustain our values beyond just survival.
Then we shall blossom.
And when the wild time is tamed,
the springboard is set for us to explore...
to commit and find our dreams.

Smile

Did you even smile today?
Did your day go your way?
Or did the hassle and the noise make you throw out all your toys
from the metaphorical pram?
Did you love your fellow man?
Did you holler, did you scowl? Did you sulk and did you howl?
Shout at innocents along the way?
So, then, not a good day today!

We are in charge of our emotions, let's not connect to the
        commotion
that goes throughout life all the time.
Let's choose our own tunes, make them rhyme.
And if they don't match others close,
let's move away, not be verbose;
instead of words that sting like whips,
let's lift the corners of our lips.

Examine carefully the perception, change the situation
with a smile upon our faces we shall see the correct places
to find ourselves encompassed in;
then we're on the up, then we can win.
A simple smile upon the face can make the world a happier place.
Let's not reject it with the mind, but if we try perhaps we'll find
how much life changes with simple actions,
and so few difficult distractions;
from day to day life will improve.
No need to let go or remove the complications that bring you down –
it's simple really, change that frown!

Be aware what others perceive, as what you give you will receive.

Angry?

Don't shout and scream and stamp your feet,
just smile at everyone you meet;
there is no point in anger now,
so hear me as I show you how.

Lift your lips, it makes a smile
and makes you go that extra mile
to ease your ire and make you calm.
It really is a soothing balm.

Being angry will achieve
nothing; so relieve the stress
by listening to the inner voice.
We always have another choice!

Feel The Love

Let's make our ancestors proud of us, and not be negative or mean,
or all they will have worked for will be lost and never seen.
Let's strive in life for the good of love and make it all we can:
peace on Earth, goodwill to us and all our fellow man.

All we have to do is try, and if each one plays their part,
opening the mind and letting love come from their heart,
then they'll see love in all its light, in many forms and ways,
which will expand and grow and give us peaceful days.

Let's apply this logic every day in every part of living,
making it the measure of our receiving and our giving,
remembering that Spirit loves us, so we never act in haste,
then the love that we are given will never go to waste.

If we close our hands together, pressed towards the chest,
this is the pose of prayer, and to say 'Namaste' – blessed;
it is a spoken valediction, an offering in a word,
and we can then be sure that every prayer is heard.

Say it all around, to everyone you meet,
no matter where they come from, it will be to all a treat,
a sign that we can learn from them, an opening of a door
that bring us so much happiness, much love and so much more.

We can always make that choice, to live in love or fear,
and if we choose the former it will bring a happy tear;
but if we choose the latter we shall not have learned the fact
that Spirit is always with us and our lives are always tracked.

Let us use our salutations to greet the world as one,
then we shall find that all the pain and all the fear has gone.
Let's do a little every day and start the journey now,
for Spirit walks alongside us, trying to show us how.

Trust their judgement now and take on board their peace,
this is the way we can achieve the slaying of the beast
that haunts us all in all we do, pushing us off track,
making us feel inadequate, thinking of all we lack.

Don't give up on the game of life for in lands both far and near,
each of us is the same, we live in love or fear.
Don't leave it until it's too late, for our Spirit friends above
know that the only way is for us to feel the love.

Meditation

Find the peace and go your way, do it now, try today,
Don't sit and fiddle with your thumbs for tomorrow never comes!
It's easy just to sit and think, your mind bringing you to the brink,
it has you in its sway again, so many thoughts of there and then;
this happens to you every day, but don't give up, let's find the way.

Each and every day take time, a moment just to be sublime,
to go into your mind, go deep, jump in and take that extra leap
so you can go to places new, places created just for you
where you'll find the answers right, a special place of peace and
     light
where reason will come into view and you realise the depth of
     you.

Perhaps you'll see a lovely beach, a place that now is out of reach,
or find a forest in the sun where all is calm and work is done,
or maybe there's a favourite place that seems beyond both time
     and space…
It doesn't matter where you go, your mind will lead you, let it
     show
you where the Spirit can hold sway. It's up to you to find your
     way.

You will experience in this space all the love and all the grace
that you deserve, you should receive, do not doubt it, just believe.
You are as you should be right now, everything is right somehow,
so just remember you're the light and you can make the wrongs all
     right;
everything is fixed right here. You deserve this so have no fear.

Pay attention to all you see, hear and experience on the journey of
     'me',
for this is the spiritual path for you to enhance the beauty of your
     view.
Allow the love to come to you, feel that love in all you do
when you come back from your trip and life may surprise you just
     a bit;
you'll have new insight now and then, you'll see the love in other
     men...
And you may want to go there all the time, but we can't always be
     in such dream time;
we have normal life, but its helps to know we can return when we
     choose so.

This becomes the point in all you do, it engages and it strengthens
    you
in living the life that is only yours, opening and closing many
    doors.
There will be love, there's always pain and, yes, we always fall
    again,
but that's okay as we learn to be and our minds achieve some
    mastery,
no longer slaves to anxiety, released from fear we can be free.

Going within has great effect, allowing us deeply to connect
with all the great and good around, and finding that is quite
    profound.
Where it leads us God only knows, at first we're nervous, so
    exposed,
but never worry, now there's a plan that will encompass your
    whole life span;
so go on trying to make life grand and you'll find peace, you'll
    understand.

You'll find your peace within the mind, close your eyes and you will
    find
that as you do so and make time your life will suddenly be just fine;
the problems move and fade away and though they may return
    one day
you'll know now how to overcome them, no longer dark, you
    have the sun.
You'll find the path through every maze – problem solved, you'll
    be amazed.

Take this journey to the stars, it belongs to everyone, it's ours,
right here, right now, on this Earth it is your right from your day of
    birth
to find the true you. So make some time in a quiet place and pay
    the dime!
Of course there's no need for real money, the cost is nothing and
    you'll be free,
free from the cares that holds you fast, fears of the future and pain
    of the past.

Dream

Perchance to dream the dream of dreams,
the ones with all the wild extremes,
so much to learn so much to teach…
Are they really out of reach?
I want to sink, I want to try,
I am ready, on standby?
So off I slumber at end of day,
ready for the cabaret.

I close my eyes each night and smile,
please let my body rest a while,
let me escape from life's cruel taunts,
never respite, they always haunt
my waking hours in desperate state,
so says my speeding fast heart rate.
Can I escape the dust and grime
and have a little nice dreamtime?

My mind relaxes and escapes,
my heart a little fluctuates,
my body sinks into the bed,
my energy is so widespread…
But I am not aware of this,
it just feels like total bliss;
I must escape for just a bit
until my mind sees fit.

I sink a little deeper now,
nothing will I disallow
as in this place all can be real.
In this place I strike the deal
within myself to make it clear;
I can escape the deepest fear
that lurks within the dark recesses
of my mind and its excesses.

But maybe it will never come!
We can be ourselves and not become
that fear that lurks within the space –
we walk away, it knows its place.
We choose the love and choose the fun,
talk and laugh with our loved ones,
for they can guide us where we need,
they will plant that important seed.

But does the dream make any sense?
It's all about the future tense,
the time of now and what's to come
is an illusion – don't succumb
to the imagination as it is,
it magnifies our enemies
and all the ghouls that live within,
so head up and take it on the chin.

Dispel the sad, be the happy,
don't delay, make it snappy,
ignore the dark that pulls you back,
it loves to play when all is black.
So make the dark the same as light,
dream in the day and dream at night;
these strong thoughts will ease it all,
you are in for the long haul.

In your dreams you travel far
to places on a floating star,
may see a monster in a chair,
may dance all night with a big black bear…
It does not matter what occurs
in this sleep, it just refers
to something stuck in deep recess,
something you need to redress.

No need to worry, no need to fuss,
you won't miss the big dream bus;
they can show you the right way,
might be tomorrow, might be today,
time is only relevant here,
in dreaming it can't interfere;
in dreams where you may travel far
it's transient as a shooting star.

So dream the dream, of sense or not,
it matters little, not a jot.
It may be a message from the light
or just a jumble in the night,
may be more lovely than you can say,
and may just show you the correct way...
But know that all that happens here
will be there, then disappears.

We all dream, we surely do,
and it can bring us a breakthrough;
it can make us warm and smile,
even if it's once in a while.
So make your dreams a part of you,
let them affect your waking view,
the positive will create your power,
Then every day will be happy hour.

A-ngel Team

"Angel sitting on my shoulder,
can you move this heavy boulder?"

  Yes we can, of course, with love; but will you first give it a shove?

"I can't, it's stuck it's been a while.
I just can't seem to even smile."

    Just put your hand upon it now, and talk to us, tell us how…

"Oh, I just don't know what to say,
just want to move, get on my way…"

                  Ah, there you go, you used your voice,
                  opened your mouth and made a choice!

"I just closed my eyes and made a plea –
A-Team please, let me clearly see!"

                  We will remove the boulder now; we will lead
                              and show you how….

"It moved, it moved! I'm so relieved!"

                  Of course it did, because you believed.

Paradise

Are you searching for paradise on Earth?
Seeking every day since your very birth?
Have you found it yet?
Will you take a bet
that it exists here in this place,
this sphere that holds the human race?

You search around within your life,
but nothing's there, no joy to find,
just so much trouble, so much strife,
and you can't see, you feel so blind...
Because you're searching the wrong places,
it's not in any spaces here, not in this world, yet very near...

I stopped and found that I could see,
I looked elsewhere, I looked in me.

So I ask you to do the same,
I want you too to have new eyes,
to see this life is just a game,
and never let it pass you by...
So look within and you'll discover who you really are;
yes, it's a test but you'll recover, don't settle for being under par.

Everything you need's inside,
so don't deny or ever hide
all the emotion that you feel –
that's what makes you the more real.
Let go of all that's negative,
feel refreshed and start to live,
yes, live your life with strength anew
and inner love, the real you.

You may not believe what I am saying,
you're in such a state, your nerves are fraying,
can't see the wood for the tall, dark trees,
you feel like falling on your knees…
But don't despair and don't give up,
there's an overflowing, loving cup
held in beauty by an unseen hand,
that will lead you to the Promised Land
of love and happiness, your domain,
so allow them now to take the strain.

It isn't very hard to do –
imagine them, imagine you,
joined in thought and coming near
with nothing to lose except your fear;
make the requests of what you need
and they will surely plant the seeds
to make your dreams come true –
they want the best for you!

The understanding that you gain
will very gently cause a pain within your heart,
within your soul, searching out the deepest hole…
In this place that you resist
you'll find the very thing you've missed;
in giving way to this simple act
you'll learn the most important fact,
that uncovers the greatest lie:
you cannot die.

So are we alive or are we not? Confused about reality?
It doesn't matter, live and laugh, enjoy the spiritual duality!
We're one together, can't be apart,
seen and unseen, joined in one heart,
and this is where paradise grew –
in the love between the two.

This happiness we all deserve in our life today,
accept that it is meant to be, jump in and join the fray!
Leading by example is a strain, I know, but we all must,
so never fear the pain – you won't be on you own – and trust
you never have been, nor will be, left alone without a guide.
Walk on with pride and you will see there's no more need to hide.

Walk this life in paradise,
in warmth and love; it's true –
the love you feel but can't visualise
comes on angel wings to you.
This angel will protect you forever and a day,
so be your best, forget the rest.
Together is the way.

You Are Beautiful

Do you know how beautiful you are? Do you know your worth?

So many of you do not, so many of you berate yourselves each day for not being 'good enough'. But good enough for what and for whom? All you need to know is that you are good enough for you. Everything about you is just perfect, for you.

Stop trying to fit the lives of others to your own. Choose your own version – be different. Be the champion of your destiny and the master of your own life. Take off your boxing gloves! Live in this moment, but remember all the other moments as it is those that help us.

Make the correct choices, don't try so hard, just allow it to happen. Ultimately the end result will be perfect.

If I told you, you were beautiful would you smile? So smile – close your eyes, know the truth and feel cherished.

The Angel Said To Me

"The best is yet to come, my friend," the angel said to me one day,
"I see you and I hear you when you come to me and pray.
I feel your loving emotion for those you care about in life,
I know well all the problems that have caused you untold strife.

"But it's okay, you know, to feel the things you do,
because I'm there, all the time, standing next to you.
I never take a break, I do not have to eat,
it's you who needs to listen and take a small retreat.
You run around from day to day, never stop to see what's real,
listening to all the rubbish and ignoring what you feel.

"But you have a choice to change this, if you only did believe
that I am really here and that you are worthy to receive
just what you want at any time. So ask and let me bring
what you need to be comfortable – it isn't such a sin
to have whatever you believe is right for you right now,
you just have to let go and trust me, and I will show you how.

"What you need to know right now, and for all the time to come,
is already there inside, the magic is for all, not some.
So believe in me and believe in you, believe in what will be,
what is right in love and truth and light will shine out, just you see.

"Personally, I look forward to each and every day.
I love it when you laugh and I love it when you play
for then we see the real you, the one you want to be –
the person in the mirror, the reflection that you see.

"So carry right on now, honing all your skills,
and stop fighting with yourself, that battle of the will...
For we are spirit as are you, and you'll return to the spirit world
when all your life has been revealed and the miracles unfurled."

You've Come This Far...

I feel your fear, I feel your dread, will you ever get out of bed?
Will you ever reach your goal, the one you hold within your soul?
You try so hard with every day to will the energy your way,
to bring your dreams without delay.

But never mind your human ways –
ask us, we will be there to heed
and bring the magic that you need.

The message is let go of fear,
live in the now, live in the here,
let go of that which brings you down,
the negativity in that frown,
and know that spirit leads you right –
it can work for you this very night.

So don't give up, you've come so far,
you're so close to your chosen star.
A little faith, a little push,
no need to hurry or to rush
for this was always meant to be.

Open your eyes and you will see
you are amazing, you're divine,
and you will always truly shine.
So shine your light for all to see,
this is for you and it's for me
because I love you with all my heart.
Know it was me who shot the dart
to make the link between us two –
this is the miracle just for you.

Peace of Mind

I was looking for peace of mind – it isn't very easy to find!
Is it hidden under a chair or even under the darkest stair?
Can you tell me please, anyone, for I have been so much alone?
I asked my neighbour up the street and almost everyone I meet,
they look at me most bemused – I'm now becoming all confused.

Then someone said, "Look within." I did, in my arm, my foot, my
    shin,
it wasn't there; I sighed again, I scowled a look of sour disdain.
It clearly isn't here for sure, I'm not going looking anymore,
I'm bored with this new-fangled stuff.
It does not exist. It's all a bluff.

So I stopped looking and each morning rose,
sat on the bed and stretched out my toes,
with a shake and a yawn and a small prayer
to shake off the shadows, well, maybe a layer.
I know how I work, I know what I am,
I'll no longer be the sacrificial lamb!
So with no expectations I'll just follow the path,
live in the now, leave the past with a laugh;
it's scary, I know, but I will go onward and upward, on with the
    show.

In making that choice I heard a loud voice
in my head, so loud and so clear:
"Just be who you are, in both near and far
and what is needed for you will appear."
So I looked a bit deeper and found I could see
so much further than ever –
now I must endeavour to grow and become all I can be…

29

I'm taking my time, it isn't a crime,
we all follow our paths at our own chosen speed.
Some want to be flowers, some want to be trees,
whatever it is it is all that we need
and it matters not what others may say –
in the end we're all one as we follow the way.

I share with you now all that I know
and maybe you think I know nothing at all,
but at least I have tried and I've fought, laughed and cried
and I'm still moving on and I'm still walking tall.

Have I found that peace I so eagerly searched for,
that in every place seemed hidden from me?
For the most part, yes, but I didn't look,
it just happened almost by chance for me.
I must have had help, I know that I did,
and I'm proud to be chosen for my task.
And I will give for as long as I live,
for as long as other people ask.
It's in giving and loving and sharing and moving,
we find the life that we truly need;
God is there is our heart and in every part,
it is He who planted the very first seed.
He is there if you want Him, if not it's okay,
you can live your life in your chosen way
and one day you'll see signs, they're for everyone
to know in the dark that the light's always on.

One-Liners

To love others. you have first to love yourself. You can go the way of passion – but are you passionate about yourself? Love yourself first and foremost, that is the way.

Loneliness is sometimes beautiful. Occasionally we all need the space to be ourselves, to live in our own energy, to accept the problems around us and find the peace. It is in the peace that the solutions are found.

You are not strong today – at least that is what you tell yourself – but you would be wrong. It is only your perception of the negativities around you. Stop for a second, feel the angelic presence taking them out of your energy. Smile, for you are blessed.

Winston Churchill once said, "You must never, never, never give up." He was right. If you have been led to the striving for your goal in the first place, it is divine. So let the Divine help you in your belief.

Stop striving so hard, look for signs of the sun and it will always appear.

Is the Spirit world with you? Of course they are. Their light and energy link to you as you do to them. All is one, there is no separation. You are the light.

Fight the Fight

We have all the time in the world to live our lives –
or so I thought a day ago; it's funny how things change
from what we want to what we get – not that we always know,
yet what will be will be and we must think again.

We think we know what we've planned out,
but pages we have written before we even came to Earth
give our journeys a course, bring challenges to us.
And don't I know what that means, some knocked me off the
    rails;
but I recovered, used my angel wings to hover freely
and give me oversight and clarity
to know what I needed to be me.

Sometimes I look with a pained eye – did I really choose that?
I must have for a moment been unstitched.
But apparently not, or so I'm told;
I just have to be extra strong and step out of my shell
and match the others stroke for stroke,
to let them know that I am me (in all my impropriety).
I don't care what others say, I know I'm special
and my angel knows I'll win.

It takes a battle to fight your corner, to play your score,
don't listen to the bitter words incurred,
to people who think they've done enough,
who have so much and reached perfection in the Tao…
you have to feel deep sorrow for them.
But that's the pathway that they chose
and ultimately they will lose their way a while
until they change their views and feel the love deep in their hearts.

You can only do what you can do and let it go
one day at a time to sing your song.
So many books written of the ways we chose to go.
So steel yourself for quite a ride but don't be scared
for you are right just as you are;
the plan is there and what will come will fit
when this is needed in your life.
And when you feel dazed and confused
let go of pain and smile that God is love and in your heart.

Bucket List

Do you have a bucket list, some words to show you still exist?
When are you going to start your search
for your special experiences on Earth?
Should you start when time is short or maybe you believe in
  nought?
Will you die today? Maybe yes or no
but we all will go past this plane, so what's it worth?

Are you going to try for more or settle with your current score?
Will you demand a second chance,
refusing to accept what's lost?
You'll be amused when you find you could have had it all the
  time…
So add this to your pages now
that we must try our hardest, and never count the cost.

What is it that holds you back? Is it fear of what you lack,
a fear of failure, fear of falling?
Try instead to only see the good.
You will be led, your way well guided, all your secret fears
  confided,
and all that matters is that you tried
to make your blessed dream more understood.

When we pass on, our page is seen, a list of all we've done and
  been;
and this is noted in our score,
we did not wait for timing to be right
but knew beyond all human doubt exactly what the design set out.
So don't delay with making lists,
ask for spirit to bring you light.

They will be pleased to help you achieve your dreams and all that
    you believe in
within the map you have defined for living
in this world of worry and confusion.
But Spirit want us all to know this world is just a journey, so
move on towards the light and your perfection,
far beyond a bucket list's illusion.

You're Telling Me

You tell me that each of us
has a life to live,
to grow within the shell we are,
to love, to care, to give.

So I have to be accountable
for all the stuff I say;
I have to always get it right
each and every day.

I'm in the divine plan, you say,
I'm vital to its end;
but I can't quite believe this point –
are you sure, my friend?

I cannot be replaced, you say –
are you sure you know this fact?
I don't think I'm irreplaceable
with all the qualities I lack!

The cosmic energy, you say,
causes much confusion;
so what are we on Earth to see?
It's all one big illusion!

Why should I do what you say
when you tell me there's a plan,
and I have to be a guiding light
for my fellow man?

Why me? "But why not?"
I hear you loudly cry.
"Everyone must know the truth –
you simply cannot die.

"So live this life and then the next
in the love and free,
and know that you are perfect
in the God-like energy.

"So don't take life so seriously,
laugh and let it go;
and all will be just as it should
when you go with the flow."

The Animal Inside

Don't be a snake as others are,
with forked tongue, one who slides,
be the armadillo with a shell,
and a soft centre inside.
So you can talk the talk
with the intention of the best,
and hold your head up steady
when times become distressed.

Then you can hide inside your shell
a while, and dodge the worst –
it comes at you in many ways,
be sure that you'll be cursed.
But you will also always know,
the armadillo that you are,
as you walk slowly through this life
it's all a bit bizarre.

We can all use animals we know
to describe us on this Earth:
the lion and eagle, cat and mouse
can each define our worth.
So heed the animal inside,
look close by and look far –
do you stick with armadillo
and the human that you are?

Just remember always to
be dignified in your song,
and be the noblest you can be –
it doesn't last too long,
it's over before you know it
and you will have left this plane …
Will you be able to stand and judge
yourself alongside the sane?

Don't leave it until the other side
to find your dignity;
treat everyone you meet as friends
with love and honesty.
It doesn't matter who you are
or where you're going now,
it doesn't matter what you do –
what matters is the how.

Thank You

Do you say the word enough
or just ignore such platitudes,
take for granted all you have
without a word of gratitude?
Do you give thanks for all you are
and how you've come so very far,
or do you never even see
that you are walking beside me?

Give the thanks and see the smile,
go on just that extra mile;
when you say "Thank you" every day
you'll see the miracles come your way.
To give a hug of gratefulness
never fails to address
the inadequacy that you feel
for that is never truly real.

Ignore it, let it flow on by,
ours is not to reason why;
accept with thanks your gifts – don't shrug,
just live and learn and give a hug.
Give thanks for all that you achieve,
it's time for you now to believe;
deal with your needs and others' too,
for this brings out the best in you.

You'll find your life will then allow
to show you the right way somehow.
When you decide to stand up straight
fears and conflicts dissipate,
and showing others your best measure
causes everyone more pleasure.

When you smile and give your thanks
it brings forth an angel from the ranks;
someone you can look up to,
someone who will walk with you,
allow them in to be close by,
no need to argue or wonder why!
Then feel the gratitude in your soul,
fill you up and make you whole.

Pass this on to your fellow man,
it's all part of the greater plan
to share with others, to give away –
we can do this every day.

'Thanks' is such a simple word,
so carry on, don't be deterred
or think it's unimportant, for
you may just sour a friendship more,
one you wish to hold on to,
one that will really benefit you…
So keep the love within the light
and there will be no such fight;
we are rich when we have friends,
it always leads to better ends.

Were you never taught the word
or was it that you never heard
when you were growing up this sound
that means so much to those around?
So mean it from your heart each day
and say it your own personal way,
making sure, with each gift perceived,
you give the thanks for all received.

And take care how you treat others too,
for what you give comes back to you!

More One Liners

"Close your eyes, I know you are thinking of me. My arms are around you – can you feel them? Imagine our love, we promised forever and forever it will be. I am right beside you. You are safe."

Do you think you are awkward, different or strange? Don't worry about it, so are most of the people you meet every day! Who dictates what normality is? A very interesting and wide-ranging question, which perhaps you ought to consider before you slight yourself.

Perfection cannot be reached on this Earth; that is what the Spirit world is there for – to see the result. Otherwise what would be the point of any existence?

You are holding yourself back – you know you are. Let go, let God and allow the miracles to appear in their own time. You deserve them. No need to be afraid, all is exactly as it should be.

Forgive yourself, it will only hold you back if you don't. Forgive others too for it will only hold you back if you can't. But maybe you don't really want to move forward at all? So what is it that binds you? Do you really want it in your life? Time to decide.

Always speak from your heart – it's the feeling that makes the difference.

OUR
RELATIONSHIPS

Agree to Disagree

You do not agree with me and I do not agree with you;
do you think this is all right, is it something we *should* do?
Yes, we're all made in the mould
and it's been the same since times of old.
There's been conflict for as long as I can think,
many times we've been on the brink
with words of hate and many hearts shattered,
no forgiveness in the ashes scattered.

Can we fix the disagreements in the lives we live,
learn not to take all but instead to give?
Can we be greater, give up the fight,
talk to each other and be polite?!
It's certainly a test to accept what's to be,
to stand back from control and feel more free…
Who wades into the fray? Who resolves it?
Has the fire been put out? Was it even lit?

We've been stumbling in the dark now for so long,
today's the time to change the song,
to be more understanding, to hear and to see
that peaceful change that has to be.
The powers that control us in darkness and fear
have to know that a greater power is inevitably near,
watching, advising us in what needs to be…
Let's for God's sake open our eyes and see.

Working together, on ourselves as well,
not following others' paths, having our own tale to tell;
it may not fit in with those close and their call
but by being our best, we can't really fall.
When we give in to the pressures of others around
then the lion will roar and the trumpets will sound
and pain is unleashed in a way never planned,
bringing heartache and fear in our beautiful land.

So it's up to each one which path to take.
When we're angry we must just remember to make
the peace that's so needed for all on Earth,
for we are all connected by the heritage of birth.

You Are Beautiful

What is it you're searching for?
To be 'just me' or something more?
Have you fought again today
with yourself or others along the way?

Why do you do that to yourself,
put yourself on the lower shelf –
the very place with other souls full
when really you are beautiful?

You are beautiful in your soul,
you are beautiful on your way;
so create your dream and walk your path
for we love you every day.

Can you not just feel the love
as we hold you in our embrace?
We can fix your troubled life
and put the smile back on your face.

We shall love you every day,
in every place and every way;
we shall feel you in our hearts,
and we shall never be apart.

In the darkness and the light,
we know that your future's bright;
we shall always make you smile
walking with you the extra mile.
Know this love is meant to be –
love is our only destiny.

Heal the Pain

So much pain, I feel your tears,
it's been going on for years –
I've heard you cry and heard you pray
for it all to be lifted, taken away.
But it's not for me to take away
this pain that you are feeling now;
I can't make it disappear
but I can show you how ...

Close your eyes and you will find
that loving feeling spread within;
it creeps into your silent mind
like the rustle of an angel's wing.
Don't be scared, don't be afraid,
this is the secret to be at peace –
you don't have to do a thing
this love will all your pain release.

It pours through you, a cure to find
for body, spirit and the mind;
receive it, it's sent from above
on flights of angels' love
so you can fly free, letting go
of all the problems in your life,
no need to hang on any longer –
they're right here now to make you stronger.

Now is your time to accept
the relief coming for you
from the universe, or a friend
or, yes, from a healer too.
It doesn't matter how it comes
to you, just that it does;
stop questioning the why and how –
accept it, just because.

And we shall send you healing,
gladly give it to you all
until you are completely grown,
now that you've heard the call.
It is so, shall ever be
for all your living days;
this energy that loves you dearly
will astonish and amaze.

And when you panic for a moment –
"What if I can't grow up?
What if I just can't succeed?"
We shall always fill your cup.
Stop worrying, my dearest ones,
you have no need to fear;
we love you all so very much
and we are always near.

A Mother's Love

How is this defined? A very good question and one not easily answered. We are all supposed to love our children unconditionally. We are all supposed to care enough to watch over them until they are old enough to take care of themselves – and then some.

But some cannot. Some are scared and unsure and not at all perfect, so how can we do it in that situation? I am here to tell you that all you can do is your best. We in the spirit world have no special powers, although we are often thought of as having them; no, there is often so much to do that we can't think straight. So let me tell you, everyone makes mistakes; everyone does things they are not proud of – lose their temper, for example – yet feels the love in equal measure. That is okay. So do not judge yourself too harshly, even if others do.

Children are your divine right, but some cannot physically conceive them. That is very sad, but there are always other ways to see and feel the love of a child. There are amazing scientific steps in your world these days to make that miracle happen. Never doubt that if you are meant to have a child, you will; but if you are not, you won't. It's simple really, so do not stress yourselves for all will be as it is meant to be.

Many children leave and go to the spirit world and this brings on the deepest of pain. Let me tell you, all your children continue to grow in the spirit world. Everyone is met by family and is cared for. Each one has had the necessary soul growth it needs. It's not your fault. Blame is very easy to dish out, but acceptance is much harder.

You need to know this: through all the strife and the love, the smiles and the anguish that you cause each other, you are never alone. You are guided.

And you will try to guide your children in the way you believe is right. This is good, but remember that they are not you. They have their own dreams, which may not align with yours. But have faith that all will be well in the end. Yes, they will make mistakes, and they may break apart – then you will put them back together again and send them on their way. Some will learn and some will not, and the lesson will be repeated; but that is their choice just as it is yours.

The commitment you show over many years builds a bond, a special love, and there is no other like it. The bond is particularly strong, even when one is on the other side of life – the love never dies. The love you share in your hearts is so real, so tangible, you can close your eyes and feel it. "Once a parent, always a parent and once a child, always a child." You may be both and then you are lucky and can see both sides of the coin. Your learning is never complete, it evolves over time and grows to educate you in the finer points of human nature.

So when you feel lost and despairing, when you feel that you can't go on, just ask us to be with you and ask us to be with your children. We can help. We always help. We never say we are too busy. Remember to ask help for yourselves as parents too.

Know that all is well, all is just as it is meant to be. We angels can be very human sometimes, you know. Please accept our love and our help. We have all been there before you.

A Friend

Throughout your life, what is more comfort than the love of a
    true friend,
someone who will guide you, love and laugh with you,
someone who accepts your will?
A sister or a brother or a stranger met by fate
who brings close feelings to your heart
and is always there for you.

And when there is anger and pain, will it hurt or break this love?
Remember that I protect you,
keeping your heart laughing and loving,
parting and then coming back together as one.

So wherever you go through time and travel,
you must know that this is the deal;
we can never be parted by life's distractions.
So hold tight onto that thought,
and walk on in your life with all its trouble,
knowing I will be here to ease all your fears.
I am your friend and I shall show you the way.

Broken?

You told me you would care for me. You said you would be there.
But I was just too blind to realise you didn't want to share.
You were present in body, not mind. You seemed to look through
    me.
Yes, you were caring, not unkind. But somehow unmoved, unable
    to see.

I noticed there was something wrong when you turned away from
    me.
How could you just turn your back and break my heart so badly?
The pain in your eyes, the defeat of will, the admission of the
    strain;
this broke my heart in two and tears streamed like falling rain.

Should I let you walk away? Should I fight and shout?
Or should I just let go of you and learn to live without
the love you promised to commit to me for all our life?
Now you leave me for another, though I'm your loving wife.

We built this house, this home, to bring up a child or two,
and there seemed to be such love – but you only think of you.
You just sat me down one night, well, at least you didn't lie to me
when you said that we would have to part, to let us both be free.

Our directions in our lives have grown to paths of separation
and as you talk to me of this, I feel your desperation
to leave, so go, I hope that you are all you wish to be;
I wonder if along the way you'll spare a thought for me.

Perhaps I felt the same at times but silence always won,
I never would have gone, I would have stayed `til all was done.
So now we walk alone in pain with thoughts of so much lost,
this crisis in our lives, this counting of the cost.

But I rest assured that angels know there will be so much more,
there's life and love and laughter and the opening of new doors.
I need their watchful care more now, but I feel them close, above,
I thank them for the gifts they gave,
I thank them for the future saved,
for I am me and proud and strong and I know that I am loved.

Mother Earth

Love the future that is your children. Educate them in the love that is required in your world. Teach them to care, to be concerned, for you never know when they will need that love in return. Let them understand the planet you live on. Let them know that she needs the positive energy of everyone to survive; give back to her, as she sustains you all. Earth is the mother of you all, always there for you. You can see that she has many children to take care of and not all of them are perfect, not all of them do what they are supposed to do – yet she still gives freely.

Do you hug her? Do you love her? Indeed some do, but not nearly enough. Put your hands on the ground, close your eyes and feel her love wrap around you. She has great power and has been kind to you all so far – but that may not always be the case if you don't listen. So open your hearts. You understand the love for your children, so understand the love of the Earth Mother for you, for you are her children. She is there with enormous energy to bring to you what you need.

We know this, for we link with that energy too. We know her well. We know the possibilities there that have not been tapped into yet. She does too and when the time is right she will draw you to them.

You have a choice. You have a voice too. So use it for your children, for your human self, for your spiritual self – and use it for the Earth that sustains you all. Without her you would be nothing.

We shall continue to watch over you all; we love you all. Love each other.

Brother

You brought out so much love in me,
yet you had such a destructive tendency.
You would be angry and then so kind,
with no belief in the divine
or in survival; but then you passed
and you could be at peace at last.

You'd never really felt secure,
a troubled mind that wanted more...
But you met our brother and our dad
who welcomed you with open arms,
forgiving all that you'd kept hidden
for the love you always gave unbidden.

I saw you as a sister – teased
and angry, sad and loving, pleased
that you had always got your way,
for you needed that to feel okay.
You had such a conniving smile,
choosing the right time, and while
the world revolved around your door
you fought and loved and needed more.

But would the 'more' have kept you here?
I say that as I wipe a tear
from my damp cheek... Another year?
Would that have made a difference?
Yes, we always have a preference
to leave this world at a later date
but then we must accept our fate.

You had to go, we had to part,
though never from my loving heart,
only from this world of strife
that caused your heart to fail and go
to another place, another life…
Yet closer still, where I surely know
that you are free from fear and pain;
a place within where once again
we can be strong and hug each other.

I love you still, you are my brother.

Friends?

I am your friend – are you quite deaf?
You needed me, you were bereft;
and I wanted to help you, wanted to care,
wanted so much to be always there.
But you only listened to the dark,
never saw the hidden spark
within your soul, the path of light.
You only wanted to spit your spite.

It hurt me when you turned away,
I tried to shout, I tried to say
I'm sorry you misunderstood,
you thought I wasn't any good.
I really want to punch your nose,
kick your shins and stamp your toes!
And wish for monsters in your head,
and spiders underneath your bed!

You judged me harshly, it wasn't true
what other people said to you;
But you listened `cause it suited you,
you didn't care what's false or true.
I had to get it in my head,
friendship was over, it was dead;
it's hard to swallow, hard to feel
I was so sad, didn't seem real.

But I'm not you, you'll have to find
your own way forward; don't be unkind
for I don't wish you any ill.
Go your way, it is your will.

I wish you love, for you I pray,
but I'm not going to force my way
back into your life, though you'll try…
You know you will. You'll ask me why
we can't be together as before;
yet you know well I can't ignore
things that were said between us two
and think that I shall forgive you.

Forgetting is a another thing –
I'll try though it will always sting.
I'll do my best to wipe my mind
of all the negativity I find;
and every time you say I'm wrong
I'll stand up tall, I know I'm strong.
I know I did as I should have done,
so I release the anger held within;
it's how it is, the race is run,
and when it's over no-one wins.

So this is how it has to be,
we journey on separately.
And next time you walk near my door
just keep on walking, wanting more,
walk to your future – and take your stuff
for I have had more than enough.

And so I wave you from my life
and smile, releasing all the strife,
refusing negativity like you,
trying to be kind and true.
Though when this life shall meet the next
don't be surprised if I'm still vexed!
A broken heart is hard to mend
when you've said goodbye to a so-called friend.

And I know that I'll get hurt again,
the same old lessons will remain,
but I'll grow stronger every time
for I am light, I am sublime,
I know my value on this Earth
and I know that there will be rebirth.

Soul Sister

You came into my life
to calm the waves; I didn't know
I needed you, thought I could cope,
but in you came, opened my eyes.
and I trusted you, you gave me hope,
as if we were two sides of one
or part of a soul group, you and me,
that we should meet now at this time
was somehow mutual destiny.

A diamond facet in the rough,
the path we've chosen as it seems,
pulling together in the fray,
fixing the world in whatever way we can,
to ease it for our fellow man.
We must face the world heads high
an example always to the others,
speaking the truth that never dies
to our sisters and our brothers.

To learn, to love, to live through pain
is all part of the divine plan;
we must always do what we can.
But no more need we be alone,
for we two know the love that joins us.
You are my spiritual sister now,
but I have always somehow known
you, and I'll never let you down,
never let you be alone.

Dear sister, friend, I shall return to you
all that you've given me and more;
we'll walk like angels in the light
and we'll achieve so much because
we have each other, day and night.
We have all we ever need,
together we can now succeed.

Child of Time

Children are a boon, it's said, but they never listen or get out of
    bed!
When they've reached that age when they know it all
and we know nothing, they put up walls;
  oh, kids can be so very bold, they love to tell us we are wrong,
won't ask for help when they need to hear
but they run to us when they're not strong or full of fear.

But nonetheless we love them still, always testing our iron will!
We love them as that beautiful child,
the one who was so sweet and mild;
  where have they gone, stolen away? We never did expect
the sullen face and rolling eyes, the absolute lack of respect…

How they changed just overnight, the studs, tattoos, a frightful
    sight!
The need they have to scowl and vex,
the need they have for the opposite sex…
They only needed Mum before, but now we have to step back
and watch them change in front of us and tell us what we lack.

We can't stop this transition phase, so change our tack and lavish
    praise
on them nonetheless, to keep them here, to keep us whole
while they think that they're in control!
But we are watching every day, to make sure they believe their way
is right for whoever they need to be, while trying hard to set them
    free…

He never asks for hugs these days, all he needs are the games he
  plays
as he lies on his messy bed! I wonder who's playing with his
  head...
And now I have to be a friend, I have to give, I have to bend
and let him know no matter that he wanders far
I'll be the light while he's the star.

I know this phase will one day pass, and he'll surely land on his arse
many times along the way! But this we have to do,
although it scares me through and through
to see the child, a part of me,
and want to save him from this stuff he has to be.

But it's only life and it does change, experience strengthens the
  emotion's range,
then we can cope with all the strife
that comes with growing into life.

And I see myself in him each day; it makes me smile, I know the
  way!
All those things, I did them too –
did you think it was only you?
We've all been where you are, we know the whys,
we invented the excuses that you make, and all the lies;
our mums and dads, they shook their heads in mock dismay –
for parents it's another normal day.

And when he smiles, opening his eyes, it's such a big surprise to
    see this face
so full of love as he stretches out with animal grace
and tears my heart – I thought he was about to start
a shouting match, a fight, more pain –
I smile right back and see my baby child again.

And so I stand and shake my head, '"Will you just get out of bed?"
He scowls a little and I smile,
yes, we go that extra mile
for they are part of our souls every day
and we'll protect them even when they stray.

So go, be you in whatever way you can among your fellow man
and live life to the full; my only care
is one day you will understand the love we share.
And as you age and hair recedes, and I am gone, from here
    displaced,
know that you will never be replaced
for you are the very heart of me whatever happens, still
I love you now and always will.

Brotherly Love

I dreamed of you last night, seeing you well, so alive and vibrant, and my heart ached to know that you were with me. It has been such a low time of late, and life has been such a challenge; sometimes people can be so horrible. I just needed to know that you were there.

As you held me in your arms and told me that you loved me, I became strong and alive again. You were just as you had been on Earth. You were such a strong presence when you were here, larger than life with a penchant for trouble that followed you everywhere. But you had a disarming charm and you knew it, and I loved you nonetheless, because you were my brother.

You talked of still being here, of watching me and laughing at me. You talked of strength and love and how you would protect me and it was just what I needed. I had wanted to run and hide, but now I know that's not the way. I know I should not be scared of what's to come but walk forward with a determination in my mind that I can succeed, that I can achieve my dreams. It's difficult sometimes when you're not around here to go through it with me. Sometimes I feel guilty that you're over there and I'm over here, but then I know you are content where you are and all is exactly as it is meant to be. I know you can reach out further from where you are.

Thank you for placing the covers over me as I slept; I was cold but too tired to pick them up. I felt them slip off the bed as I fell into slumber, dog-tired. When I woke and found them neatly over me I knew that you had done that and it made me hug myself indulgently. I feel lucky to have you around, my protector in life and my protector in spirit. You can't always be there, and are not always needed – just when I wobble.

When I reach my goal, you will be there right by my side protecting me still, and I shall have achieved it all for both of us. So I'll see you again, but not too soon. We have work to do.

The Best

You were my best and I was yours,
we played the game and checked the scores –
they were the highest they could be,
I belonged to you and you belonged to me.
You made me laugh so much I cried
to know our souls were so allied
in this life, we became one
and I knew my life had then begun.

You saved me from an awful fate,
coming not a day too late,
for I was sinking, then you came
lit up my heart when you called my name.
I was on the edge of falling,
in despair and calling out
for change in what had gone before;
I was wounded, I was sore.

And in you came as if Heaven-sent,
making all the bad relent,
making it just disappear,
chasing away the things I feared.
You were so very strong for me,
gaining my trust by degrees.
You just came in and loved me whole,
right down to my very soul.

I would be nothing without you.
You taught me it was worth pursuing
dreams; and in time I became
stronger with your burning flame,
My heart ignited, now it burns,
and the deepest love my heart returns.

You're so laid back and so controlled,
while I am stubborn, won't be told,
but you just smile and shake your head,
you never argue, walk away instead,
allowing me to make mistakes,
so much my heart and mind will ache –
then in you ride on your white horse
and always save the day, of course!

I may not tell you every day
that I love you, it's just my way,
the way that fits for you and me,
we don't need scenes of flattery.
Yet my love is deeper than you know
even if I do not show it,
just believe I will always be
with you through fate and destiny.

And when this life its course has run,
and we say goodbye to moon and sun,
we will be walking side by side
and nothing will have ever died.
How much time is left to go?
Let's not worry about what we can't know,
just live and laugh and be with me,
for I am your own devotee.

So thank you for always being there,
for saving me from my despair.
There's just one thing more I have to say:
I love you more with every day.

When You Have to Go

When you realise the love has gone
but cannot find the time to leave...
When did it all go so wrong?
Can it ever be retrieved?
Would it ever be the same,
the love and laughter that we shared –
is it gone in all but name
or could it maybe be repaired?

Questions follow, one on one,
but is it wise to trust them now
or should I just say that "It's done"
and let it go, restart somehow?
Is the timing ever right
for the sadness this will cause?
This could be a running fight –
maybe I should pause...

I feel so guilty, feel so sore,
thinking that it's done and gone;
but I really do want so much more
than the path we find ourselves upon.
Can we both just walk away
or will be it be too hard to do?
Should I just say that I'll stay,
forget it all and be with you?

I promised you the truth always,
but how do you ever say the fact
that far from those past halcyon days
we no longer interact?
Hardly ever together now,
we live our lives apart;
I do my thing, you do yours
and of mine you want no part.

But I do want a partner,
someone to share my heart;
fed up with feeling all alone,
I need another start
with someone who really loves me,
who cares if I am there;
someone to tell my dreams to,
someone who will share.

Perhaps I could keep the magic going,
perhaps, if we were one;
but the secret's in the knowing
that really all is done!
So I'm going to find the courage
to raise this very soon,
and I know you will discourage me –
it will not be opportune.

But I can't go any longer
without being honest to your face,
and find I'm so much stronger
now that we don't embrace.
When I'm with my friends who care,
I feel so much more blessed;
but leaving them, returning,
only makes me feel depressed.

I cannot do this any more,
I've given all I can
and if I stay here any longer
I'll be old before I am…
I do wish you the happiness
deserved for every soul,
but I have to take decisions now,
I have to take control.

There's only so much one can give
before it's time to leave,
when all your friends are telling you
there's nothing more to be achieved.
And I have put so much deep thought
into the life I want from now;
unfortunately it can't be bought
or else I'd find out how…

So taking courage, with a heavy heart,
I'll knock your door to tell you
that it's better if we are apart,
it's time to say farewell.
I've practised this so many ways,
to say these words to you;
it never gets any easier,
an awful thing to do.

But you're locked into the life you want
which no longer includes me;
I can no more be nonchalant,
so open up and see
that we would be happier apart.
I'm certain of this too;
though you'll always be within my heart,
I'll always care for you.

I'll take all that you throw at me,
the dark recriminations;
I don't expect you to agree –
I have no expectations.
Yet I thank you still for all we had
and hope you can forgive,
as I head for my launching pad –
I only want to live.

No more pretence behind closed doors,
no more inventing lies,
it's time to move on, time for more,
without wondering if or why.
Wherever my decisions take me
I'll grab it with both hands;
to live, to love, to laugh, to dream –
a life that can expand.

From Granddad

You were always special to me from the day you were born, as delicate as a flower and as strong as I have ever seen. You did things your way – which was not approved of by others – but you did make us all chuckle.

The day your father died, I had to stop you from rushing to him. I had to keep you back, you didn't want him to go, and that broke my heart; but there was no-one else to do it and then for a while you wouldn't come to me. You felt that I'd broken your trust and for that I am sorry.

I tried to live a good life and my family was everything to me. It was all I knew. But grandchildren bring a whole new perspective into it when they arrive, as you now know. Really, you would like nothing more than to be with them all the time as they really give a new focus on life. There were seven grandchildren and we loved them all; but you were the youngest and needed us more.

It's true that when I passed over I thought I wasn't ready for it. I missed so many things. I missed our cuddles. I was surprised when I reached this side because it's not how I thought it would be at all; but it is worth all that happens in life to be here.

I watched you from here and I came to visit you unseen as soon as I could. When the opportunity came for someone to appear to you, I stepped forward; we believed it would be too much for you to see your Dad – the wound was too raw back then. So I came when you did not expect it. That is usually the way and I stood in all my solid form and smiled at you. I felt your fear and I was sad about that. I tried to let you feel me but you couldn't let down the barrier then and you ran away. You felt such shock that we decided to make you rest for a while, and you slept while we helped you process your experience. I came back several times after this and was seen often. I became quite good at it!

You see, I am always helping you in your life. When you think of me, I am right here beside you, puffing away on my pipe and listening to your thoughts, seeing you doubt yourself, berate yourself. All I can say to you is to remember where you have come from and how hard it once was. At least you will not have all that again. What matters is now and that is what you must concentrate on. I can see how we all plan ahead, how we think tomorrow should be arranged – but you can't, you don't know what tomorrow will bring. You don't know what choices will be made and who will affect them, not until it happens.

When you need me, I will be there. When you are searching, I will be there to open the door and help you see clearly; and when you fall I will pick you up, dust off your knees, hug you and send you onward. When it is time to come over, I will be waiting at the door as I always did when you came home from school; is that not where you have come from? It will be like old times, yet the times will be new and full of so much promise. One day, I promise, we will hug again and laugh again and the journey will all have been worth it.

Never think that I do not agree with who you are. You have made me so proud in the work you do and I come to see you often. You have you mother's flair; however, your grandmother thinks you take after her! But I know that you are just you, in all your beautiful glory – sometimes too trusting, though you give your all to others for the benefit of so many on this side of life and that side of life. Long may you continue.

God bless you, my beautiful granddaughter. And for all the beautiful granddaughters everywhere – know that your grandfathers watch over all of you.

Teenagers

The teenager is a problem, an enigma to be solved –
how do we control them ? How did they evolve?
We all believe our youngsters are the best there's ever been,
but let's take off the blinkers and see what must be seen ...

Control is not the way, although you ask and plead and beg,
and think they need a life like yours – then they just pull your leg.
They are all individuals though you may not like their ways,
hanging round with trouble, sleeping through the days ...

Sometimes you would love to walk away from all the stress,
but in your heart you know you can't, however much the mess!
One minute you shout a curse at them, next they look forlorn,
so then you have to hug them though it only brings you scorn ...

They think they're very clever, telling you fib after fib,
but you know this and it makes you smile, you know you will
        forgive them.
Sometimes your head may just explode, you can't always be strong,
when they always seem to get their way and never admit they're
        wrong ...

Just a short, short time ago they were the model child
and you were proud to show them off, smiling, meek and mild;
then, God, how did it happen that my child turned into this?
I cannot for the life of me think how it went amiss ...

But I am told there's hope for us and as the years progress
they will become responsible. I don't quite believe that yet,
for several years have come and gone with no sign of any change
and I wonder if mine's different – it's really very strange ...

I do want him to be happy, I love him with all my heart,
he is the life and breath of me, my perfect work of art.
But I don't know how to help him now, don't know what's for the
     best;
it might help if, by the afternoon, he'd get up and get dressed…

So I've decided to step back and leave it up to him to live;
whatever he gets up to now, I've little more to give.
Of course, there's hugs and love and words and meals by the
     score,
but whatever else he needs from now – he'll just have to
     explore…

I know him better than he does, I know his hopes and fears,
he's told me all these in his eyes through the preceding years.
And I hope he can confront the demons that nearly make us
     blind,
that they drive him to his purpose and not out of his mind…

And I hope he can remember those who always love him still,
no matter what he fights against, no matter what his will.
And I hope he'll be all that he can, a brilliant purpose find,
remembering to be caring, remembering to be kind…

So I'm not going to fight with him and I'm not going to shout,
it will only make him angry and determined to walk out,
so we'll agree to disagree and I'll give him the space
to find the way, God willing, to join the human race…

For My Friend

I want to write a letter to my friend. I have to say that we started this friendship in a very unconventional way, meeting through spirit when you lay in the darkest of places with your heart torn to shreds. I know you didn't like me at all when we met and you kept away from me because of that; but time and again I was told you would return. Time and again, I was told to contact you to tell you I was thinking of you, though I know you did not believe that to be the case. And still you resented me – I don't know why, you never said. But I persevered.

You came back to the teaching circle because you knew you were meant to be there. Spiritual things frightened you, the feelings you had frightened you. The deep hole you were in was your home ever since your husband, your love, your soul mate had gone to the spirit world. He was too young, yes, but he had to go for you to flourish and grow – that seems like a strange thing to say, as I know that you would rather have him here. But this was about him, and this was his pathway to choose. He chose you all the way. He was so scared to move on and also scared to stay where you were.

Then you came back to me and your lovely husband started to talk to me – but I couldn't tell you. You would not have believed me. You were not ready to hear it.

Most weeks, you sat in the energy just listening to everyone else and not saying anything. I kept a special eye on you. You were my 'project', to bring you into the light for you deserved that. During those evenings, I know you started to understand, to absorb what was truly happening around you and you started to blossom. Your love of nature and the Earth was evident from day one and the fact that you have now found your shamanic side is no accident. Your understanding of earth energy and the power it contains is wonderful, and using this has now brought you to a place of great learning. The future can be scary and unexpected.

You have the most amazing spiritual abilities; contacting me through the 'spiritual airwaves' was particularly enlightening. I remember the first time it happened – how you were there when I needed you, and it's just getting stronger. I personally find it hard to rely on people and that is what I feel I am here to learn – to fix – but you have laughed with me, cried with me, kicked me and supported me. You are the mother hen for so many, as you love to fix things too. So it is a journey of fixers who support each other through the painful journey in this world we find ourselves in. The healing you give by using your animals is beautiful and you love to heal. You give to others even when they don't know you are doing so; but I do, I see it, I feel it as we are connected way beyond this world – I know you know that too. You were sent to me as much as I was sent to you.

The future will be particularly challenging for you, realising that you must not be alone on this journey and that you will have to let your husband fly free. You will have to join with another and I know how much that scares you. Whoever this is will have to match you and to be very special. Their connection to nature and the Earth will fit you like a glove and you will show your full self – nothing will be hidden as it is now. It makes me laugh when people are around you because they have no idea what and who you are, and that is just the way you like it – being incognito. But not for much longer. Soon you will have to stand up and be counted as your pathway demands it.

Every day, your words of love and care make many others smile, and you say them no matter how you feel. You say them to offer help and to give love and that is all, expecting nothing in return; but you should know that we do send much back to you, for you need it too. No-one can know what it is like to walk in your shoes and that's the same for all of us. No-one knows the pain that you have experienced; we can all imagine it but it's not the truth. We always like to think we can see others' truth, but it's the truth within ourselves that we have to acknowledge before we can cope with that.

That said, you really annoy me sometimes because you want to jump ahead and then you miss things. You have to wait for your life to unfold in the way it must. Then you panic because you realise you're not in control; but you never have been – we all have to surrender to the will of the spiritual magic, whether we know it or not. I'm sure I annoy you too as I never listen to anyone on the Earth! However, you have learned that the trick is to invade my thoughts and talk to me there. You are very crafty sometimes.

So what will the future hold for us both? Well, I don't really know. I do however know that we will work together at some point. I do like your energy when we're together, it's so very different to mine and joined together it just works; it fits and is very powerful. We do have the capability to change lives, which is our purpose, to give, to receive and to love. So when you are fulfilled, your power will be strong and you will fly together, you and your partner (with your husband by your side). I look forward to that day as I will know what you have achieved.

For all your troubles, you humble me and inspire me to be better. You are genuine and lovely and strong and I thank spirit every day since I met you. I hope that I inspire you too, as much as you inspire me. So wave your wand and raise your magic. Use it in the darkest places to shine a light; it's what we do best. I trust you and love you and I hope that the world eventually sees the real you, the beautiful you.

I have met so many people in my life who have become

wonderful friends at once. So it will always be, but then fate draws us apart and that has made me sad on many occasions. People are brought together for the time that they are needed, where there is a benefit on both sides. Sometimes that can make us sad. So I want to say that I hope we stay close for longer than a season. I hope we can still laugh and have the fun we do for years to come. I hope that the work we do will make a difference to the world and also to you; may you find all you deserve because you are worthy of it. I also lost someone in order to find this path as you have too, so together we are much stronger. We help each other cope on our bad days, and on our good days we laugh. I don't know if there is place for anyone else because you understand me so well. But know this – I will be there all your life and, even if you move away from me, our hearts and spirits will be forever entwined.

This letter is for my friend. I hope it may inspire you to send a hug to your own friends, the people whom you meet suddenly and whom you just know and feel comfortable with. These things are meant to be, so love your friends and cherish them and they will do the same for you in return. Your partnership will be blessed and you will both be loved in ways you can only imagine. It is not an accident that you met when you did; there is always a reason, so trust in that and enjoy your journey.

Always

I could never leave you.

My heart was always connected to yours by an invisible silver string.

It frequently got entwined with yours, and with others, but yours was the only one that never tore.

Yours was the only one that mattered, when I looked into your eyes and our souls met six feet up.

There was no other match on this Earth to compare.

I see your silver string trying to find me.

I see your heart heavy with pain.

But the issues that bind you are of no real consequence; you are just trying to find the connection.

The connection will always be there.

Never lose hope.

There will be other silver strings, each bringing what you need when you need it.

But we will always be together.

I love you.

Thanksgiving

There's so much that I'm thankful for,
from all the people gone before –
my Dad, my friends, so many others,
especially my lovely brothers
who watch over me each day.

And I pray that I can change
some things in this world to bring
more pleasure and, yes, more delight,
bring folks together in the light
of many possibilities.

For all who share this lovely place
and all who dwell in time and space
who sacrifice so much for now,
I pray we can remember how
to rejoice always in our living,
and never forget the thanksgiving.

Value

I value myself now and understand the choice
I made to speak my truth and learn to use my voice.
It's never easy to fight this lonely cause
and learn to be oneself without a pause.

To my surprise, my shame, I realised
that I was always as I am and that I must
be proud of who I have become and will be,
for in the end we shall return to dust.

So I hope and trust, go on believing,
and try each day to strengthen me,
accepting all experience
is meant to be.

I fail most days, the darkness holds me
in its sway; but I have learned
that I must never give up, knowing
every shadow one day turns.

And you are my reward, my love.
I never knew that I could love
as strong as I do now
and from this day I vow
to always be standing by your side,
whether unseen or unknown,
for it was you who turned the tide
and you will never be alone.

It's taken time, it wasn't overnight,
the journey has been great to know
just who I am, but worth the tears
to find you and release my fears.

We'll guide each other now and for all time
we'll always hold the keys to one another's heart;
the past lets go, the future becomes now,
we walk together and will never be apart.

A Spirit's Love

Today I told you that I loved you so many times but I don't think you heard me; at least you never acknowledged it. I do that every day in the hope that you will know and come to understand that I do.

Who am I? Who do you want me to be? Your dreams belong to you and together we are united in the realm where only love matters. It overcomes all other emotions. Only love belongs.

You know me and you don't know me, all at once. I am a part of you as you are a part of me; that is why I love you so very much and that is why I am always here. So close your eyes and breathe, relax your body, relax your mind, relax into me and let the tendrils of my essence gather around you. Let my arms hold you near and let me kiss your cheek in reverence of your complete beauty.

I truly am here and I want to tell you how special you are and how I can help you to achieve your dreams. Listen to the winds that ebb and flow around your soul, teasing you and leading you to more. Reach for them. Take them to your heart and be loved.

Taken For Granted

In each life there will be someone who is taken for granted. We don't mean to do it but it's usually someone very close. We become so wound up and embroiled in our own problems that we assume that everyone around us will stay stable and will always be there. But often this is not the case. Everything is transient and that is how it should be. So why don't we understand that this is happening?

We cannot possibly know what is to come each day but we do know that new situations will occur and they will affect one or more of us at any time. So we should think ahead and try to remember this. We may be trying to juggle situations and fix things, but we mustn't forget 'the glue' that holds it all together – and that it may just vanish at any moment. We must make sure our glue is well looked after, that it is as strong as it can be, and knows how valuable it is!

It's not a thought that most of us consider often and most of us would deny that we take other people for granted, especially those close to us. But we do. Some are hurt and some just accept their lot, while some go out of their way to tell their loved ones how much they are cared for. The point is that none of us know how long we will be on this Earth, so rather our very dear loved ones knew that they are loved – even if it is sometimes hard to tell them. We must do so, for we may not have the chance in this life again.

I know someone who insists their partner always says goodbye when they go out – always. She tells me that she never knows when she is going to see him again, and there may be a very long wait. She makes a conscious effort to hug him and say goodbye each time he goes to work. Is this something you do?

Or have you just waved goodbye only to find that you never get the chance to hug your husband, child, parent, brother, sister or friend again? It's a painful thought and a more painful reality. I know what it feels like. Although there is spiritual awareness in my life, there are also human flaws just the same as everyone else – and the pain is just as fierce.

We all make mistakes, of course we do, it's natural and it's part of the journey. But let's not make the mistake of not telling someone we know that we love them. And if we feel the pull to call someone, even if we have not done so for a while, we should do it. How will we feel if that person were never to be seen again? Could we cope with that? When they have left this Earth, we would torture ourselves with negative thoughts of anger and guilt, and that cannot be good. So let's call our friends and call the family we love to tell them how special they are. Let's arrange to meet up; and if anything needs fixing, let's do it. Let's do it now without delay. We must not allow our ego to tell us what do, but let love guide us for this is the overriding emotion.

If we take others for granted then we shall have regrets. And regrets are very hard to turn into acceptance. Some people never manage it and are plagued for years by 'if only'. So let's tell people how much we value them by giving a gift, saying 'Thank you' or giving them a hug. Not only will it make them feel good, it will make us feel good too. And if they were not long for this world, then that is a beautiful parting gift to give someone.

A hug is a unique gift. We should share as many as we can so that when we go we will be full enough to keep going until we meet again. Let's all check our glue and make sure that it knows its value.

FOR TIMES OF
SADNESS

Promise

What will take it for you to believe in yourself? What words of comfort will you allow yourself to hear that will make a difference? There is so much heartache and pain and seeing it through can take all the strength you possess. But fear not and do not doubt that your level of strength is more than you ever knew it could be.

Your day may have taken a very unexpected turn, making you feel like your world is falling around you… but that is just not the case. Your true light is so much stronger than you can understand. Believe in yourself and use that light to find your worth and your value. Know that it is so much more than you currently think.

You have already been through so many physical problems and you have always recovered. You have done it. There is always light in the darkest of corners – maybe just a glimmer, but follow it until it leads you into the sun. It may be raining outside, but keep going and do not allow the tears to rain inside.

This journey may not be easy, but there will be nothing you cannot cope with. And when you arrive at your promised destination, all the effort, determination and faith will be worth it and you will smile. So close your eyes, breathe calmly and let us lead you to the life and the love you deserve.

So Sorry I Had To Go

I had to leave you, it was my time.
I was not sorry to go, but I know those left behind are sad.
It's okay – I have not really gone anywhere, I am still around you,
still near your beating heart.
We may not have had perfection, but it was the best that I could
   do –
the way I had to be this time around – so please don't think too
   badly of me.

I have not been here long, but I can already see that I am home.
It is where we all really belong and I am so glad to be out of that
   body,
happy to be free; I know that now I can be who I really am.
So I can help and encourage you to be who you need to be…
giving you the courage and strength to overcome your fears,
to move forward and achieve your dreams.

You are here for a long time yet, so we have plenty of time –
much of it to use for the benefit of others, but mainly for you.
I love you.
I always have.
We were always meant to share our human space,
So now I share my love with you, for the heavenly space.

Angel wings wrap around our souls and keep us together
for as long as we need one another.

Leaving This World

Take my hand in yours, lead me to the light,
for the world is getting darker and I am losing sight;
yet I feel you near me as I walk along this way
and, though I cannot see you, I have known you every day...

Oh, I'm feeling just the same as when I lived some moments
    hence,
in another kind of world, with a different kind of sense.
Now should I stay or should I move on? I realise I don't care,
it's just wonderful to know that there is more to 'over there'.
I'm curious to see what's next and if there's any more –
and then I feel a force that takes me onwards through a door
into new life, a world that simply takes my breath away
as I let go of my heaviness and welcome a new day.

I go into a hospital, a place of mirrored glass,
a place of peace and beauty where I let go of the past;
I feel a warmth and comfort and I am surprised to see
such LOVE surrounding us in here, a God-like energy.
It's not easy to adjust at first, it's taking me a while,
but then I get the hang of it and cannot help but smile
for it's just like tuning a radio to get the airwaves clear –
then suddenly I realise that I am really here!

My vision becomes lighter and clarity returns,
I'm feeling so ALIVE and now the need to see more burns in me.
I want to leave this place right now, I want to see it all –
I know that everything I need is here within my calling.
For the first time since arriving, my eyes light up with glee
for right here by my side I clearly see my family;
they're all so very happy, they're smiling and content,
and I cannot but be grateful for this moment, Heaven-sent.

I'm happy and I want to hug them close for all I'm worth –
and yes, I have a body just like when I was on Earth;
I can laugh and cry and touch, be just the same as I was before.
I AM the same as I was once, but now with so much more.

"So take your time, do what you need, you are accepted here;
this is a world forgiving so let go of all your fears.
You've left the world of sin and you've been given second birth –
and YOU will judge whatever faults you had upon the Earth.
It's really not so bad, it's only up to you,
to look at what you've done in life and what you wished to do;
just accept the truth that you are not a perfect soul –
for now you have the chance to put it right and set new goals."

This is a revelation! My whole life can now be seen,
the things I did, the people hurt and all that I have been;
I know that I can change things, I know that healing's near,
now that every moment of my life before is clear.
And I'm free to travel where I wish, in a body made of light,
through worlds that are incredible, through morning and through
    night,
crossing over continents at a smooth and easy rate –
such a pity that I couldn't do this earlier, always late!

There's only one great sadness in this lovely, bounteous plane:
I miss the people left behind and I do still feel their pain.
I cannot touch their faces, feel the warmth of being there,
and I want to tell them that I miss them, that I really care…

"Well, you have a secret weapon – you can come and go at will,
            and you can see them any time you like, but still
         we know it's not the same; you have to find another way
            to make your presence known, to make them hear
                    what you will say,
      maybe speaking through a medium or making little sounds,
            try a gentle touch or move some things around!
      Sit upon the bed at night and give them calming dreams,
         help them understand that all is not quite what it seems
         and all the worries that they have, in the world of things,
         can easily be brushed away by the touch of angel wings."

I have such opportunity to grow and live and learn
so much more than life before, I've got another turn
to be all that I want to be in this amazing land –
thanks to those who walked with me and gently took my hand.
If only I had realised that when it's time to go
there's so much to look forward to, so much more to know;
there's no such thing as death, so just let go, no need to fight,
turn away and leave the world, walk towards the light!

Loss

I did not want you to go, but you did and now my heart has broken and I don't think that I shall ever recover. You told me all was well and I believed you, but now you're gone and my heart can hardly bear the pain.

Tell me how to overcome this. Tell me how to move on from here. I close my eyes and wish you close, almost feeling your familiar presence, refusing to let you go from my mind, wanting to keep your image clear and precise and familiar. But it's just not the same as having you close, laughing at me and with me.

I am bereft, I am lost and I need you to show me the way. I believe you can. I have hope that you will, because I just don't know how to live without you.

I thought I felt you with me the other night. I am sure I could feel you as I lay drifting between the worlds. You were alive and vibrant and you held me and talked of dreams and hopes to come, told me that I will be amazing. I don't feel amazing. I can't feel anything and I don't want to be like this.

I don't know how to move on. I don't know what to do.

You always told me that the greatest journey starts with the first step, so I suppose I just have to take that step. But not now, not at this moment as I am just drifting inbetween the worlds again to a place where you are, where I can feel you and where we can be together.

Love me and give me the courage to take those steps, to find me again.

Hello!

I hear you calling me every day, when times are rough. They seem to be like that all the time just now. You become so wrapped up in the physical moment that you forget you are not going through it alone. I would never leave you.

Yes, I had to leave the Earth suddenly and it was as much a surprise to me as it was to you, trust me. And I know I wasn't perfect either but, hey, I was consistent. I was who I was and you loved me nonetheless and never judged me when others did. In return I loved you, I always did. I loved you with all my heart, you were my everything and you still are. My fault was that I never told you that very often and I regret that.

I see you struggle without me. I see you cry alone and I feel your pain. I should have made you stronger, should have encouraged you more to be yourself; but you were giving so much to so many others that you didn't seem to need it. But now it's time to listen to the little voice that's speaking quietly in your mind. I know it's hard to listen to the spirit. I never did so what am I talking about? Well, now I have some authority to talk about this since I'm here. I can help. We can help. But you have to ask your spirit friends to help – we have to be invited in.

I saw you the other night in bed, thinking of times gone past and how tough they were. You were thinking about being loved again, about maybe being alone for the rest of your life. I felt very bad then. But let me tell you now that this will not happen; there will be someone who comes and who will pull at your heart strings and worship you as it should be. I wish you that.

Perspectives are very different from this side of the veil and now I can see everything in its entirety; this is beautiful and real and where we all actually belong. I know I never talked about this stuff when I was with you; I never even believed in it, but rest assured I do now!

So I am with you when you want me to be. I am in your life and in your heart. When you don't want me, I shall go – it's quite simple. But for now just know that all is well. Go with the flow. Trust me, have faith in me and in all of us here. We can help to bring you your miracles.

Chin up, my love, your precious angel is watching over you.

My Dog

As I sit by the fire, quietly, alone,
I see where you lay and know that you're gone.
No more licking my toes, no more chewing the chair –
how I shouted at you – and no more carpet hair...

My heart feels so heavy, you were my best friend,
my everyday pal, who would run end to end
of the field we were walking, then round all the trees
as I vainly gave chase and then fell to my knees
with no breath in my body to laugh or chastise...

But now your breath is gone and tears fill my eyes
to recall how I seethed – you would not do as told,
but were lively and cheeky and always so bold.
I never imagined you wouldn't be there,
never believed I could feel such despair...

Since a pup in my pocket, I loved you for years
as I trained you – or tried to – through laughter and tears;
and my faithful friend with those brown eyes so wide
took care of me too, lying still by my side
when I was ill or upset and I needed some care.
So much fun, so much love, so much life we have shared...

But then the time came when you cried through the night
and I looked in your eyes but could see little light;
I knew in my heart you were ready to leave
so I had to let go, I had to believe
that those gone before you were waiting above
with a welcoming home, filled with such love.

You will live in my heart and my mind every day
as I walk in the fields and remember our play.
And when it's my time, I'll be with you once more
to join in the fun that you're having for sure.

So I take to my sleep and hope for sweet dreams,
knowing that life is not how it seems;
and though you're not here as another day ends,
you may be a dog, but you're still my best friend.

My Dad

It has been so long since you left me, so long that I have not laughed with you or hugged you. I miss you every day with a hunger that cannot be sated by any other person on this Earth.

I was very young when you died, but even at that young age you were my everything. My life revolved around you, my heart was matched with yours in every way. When I sat in your lap and you held me, I felt so safe, protected and loved. I remember your eyes, the way you looked at me, and when I look in the mirror now I see them looking back at me. I never imagined there would be a time when you would not be with me.

You took to your bed for a few months before you died. I knew you were ill but I didn't know how badly, I was not told. Well, how do you explain to a young child about death? Yet a child in this situation still wants and needs that knowledge. I wanted to understand but nothing was said. So I continued to lie with you on the bed, never wanting to be any other place, just accepting, your arms around me for hours.

The day came when you passed. There have only been a couple of other days like it, when my brothers came to join you. The pain that shot through me then tore me apart and broke me into pieces that took a long time to fix. I was not allowed to go to your funeral and I was suddenly supposed to carry on… But how? What was I to do without you?

It seems strange now that all through the years since then I didn't think you were with me – I thought you'd left me. The one person who would have been there didn't seem to care. I was very angry for a long time; it would have been good to talk to someone, to have had some explanation, but none came from anyone.

These days, I know you are with me. These days, you live in my heart and I feel that old familiar love very close and it makes me smile. Some day we will be together again as we belong. We need to be close to one another and it occurs to me that we must always have been, for our souls are entwined. So Daddy, hold me close as I hold you now. Walk by my side in the light of love, in the light of spirit, and know that all is well. We are together.

I Miss You

As you lay there in the dark and the tears flowed, didn't you know I was holding your hand? Didn't you realise that the love I had for you was still there?

I know how much you miss me. I know you want to feel me next to you. I want that very much too. Close your eyes and reach out for me. I am there, just a short way from your heart. I can feel it beating. I can feel so much more about you and I can hear your thoughts. Feel me as our souls touch and join together in the deepest love. Hold me.

Tell me your pains, your troubles, for as long as you wish. Let's make it forever – or is that not long enough? No matter what happens, the love we have will never diminish in any way. I cared for you so much in the physical world and I do so still. I am not helpless, believe me, I just have another way to show it now. But it is just as positive.

So hold out your arms to me and I shall walk into them. I shall hold you and never let you go.

Missing

I cannot eat, I cannot sleep, I weep
for you my love, my missing heart is torn apart.

You swore that you would never leave,
always believe in the love we had created over so much time.
We danced our tune and every day
it played for us, but now I find you've gone another way.

You promised always to be by my side.
I loved you dearly but you only loved me merely
as a passing fancy, so it seems.
And now I stare at broken dreams.

What am I to do today? Should I go or should I stay?
I can't think, I'll flip a coin and do whatever fate decides
because I have to make some choices,
even though I cannot voice them yet.

Now you're apologising for the pain?
I really don't want that again, can't listen any more
to pleading lies. You crossed your heart and hoped to die
and I would fall for every word,
so many promises for life ahead I heard.

How do I cope now, what must I do?
Yes, I am bereft, I really did believe in you;
but I shall cope, I'll find another
and a truer love to share my life.
I'll not give up on my desires nor fail to feel
because of you and what was never real.

Clarity will come with hope and smiles,
I'll walk the miles and take my journey on
to meet my soul mate.
Ours was just a path we had to travel day by day, unravelling
the mystery of life.
So go your way!

Hope

Tell me, how have you survived?
Tell me what you did to make it through.
Did you think you were alone? That I was not there?

How could you doubt me?
The love that was there before has never gone away.
I am connected to you through love, the most beautiful emotion of our Earthly life.

And love will be brought to you by many others, in many different ways throughout your life. It will be love that lifts your heart, your soul and your mind, and devastates you in equal measure.

Be inspired. Don't give in to the illusions all around you. Never give up. Listen to my heart beating close to yours, for it is one and the same.

We can never be apart.

Loneliness

Each day we are surrounded by so many people, so many different souls; some we like and some we don't like and that's okay. So many people – and yet we still sometimes feel lonely. Why is that?

Friends contact us daily or weekly and ask us how we are. We tell them what they want to hear and then all goes silent because they don't fill in the gap we feel; they do not ease the empty feeling inside. It's easy to relate to that feeling and embrace it. In some ways we should, but we must never let it consume us. We must make sure we know its place, because once it overtakes our emotions then we own it and it becomes more than it should be.

We do have a tendency to exaggerate the problems of life, it's true, but then the way one person feels in a situation is different to another. For one thing, we cannot assume that everyone has the level of learning needed to cope with an issue. Again, even though an individual does have the same learning we have experienced, they may not feel the same. We can't judge the level of feeling any other person has. We only know what we feel, even if we don't know how to let it go or express it. Maybe for a while it is necessary for it to be there, to show us the way forward; even difficult feelings and situations can sometimes be a blessing, making us look at the world differently.

Different is good. It denotes change and change is a positive step even if we deem it to be painful. The change needs to come from within us as we start to identify how we feel, as we see for example who cares and who does not, whom we want in our lives and whom we don't. Some situations take people away while others bring the people in who need to be around us at this time; but we have to pay attention to the details for the meaning is always contained there.

Loneliness is usually nothing to do with anyone else but oneself. We are almost never alone, so how could we be lonely? We should try to accept ourselves as we are, not look in the mirror and dislike what we see. Rather, love it! Love it for all that we are. We are not perfect for sure, but that does not make any difference – none of us are perfect on this Earth, not one person. That should make us feel a little better. The conflict is usually within ourselves and we have to feel a contentedness within ourselves first before we can we feel content with our fellow man. It is there, I promise, but we do have to look for it inside.

Then we must feel it, find the confidence and smile on the inside and on the outside, even if we don't feel like it. We must keep trying – faking it until we make it, but never giving up. Within us is all we need for our lives, an incredible capacity for love and strength for ourselves and for others. We all have it so we must let it flow, let our love love us. We must not allow ourselves to believe no-one loves us – it's just not true for we are always cherished and protected. It just takes a certain frame of mind to accept that, so we should search it out and hold on to it with all our heart. Look within and we will never go without.

The love we need is maybe to come, maybe in our life now, or maybe past and living on in our mind. But when we leave this Earth we take with us only the experiences of this life, the memories and the love we have experienced. So we should believe in our love, our magic, and make it a good life!

Lost?

Have you wandered off alone and lost your way?
Walking in circles, nothing sure, not even
what you're looking for …
a little peace, the strength to say
"Please help"?

Some quiet, familiar voice once in a dream
told me there are guides
and others with me by my side
and I'm part of their team
it seems.

They're always there to ease my soul,
to lift me out of loss and pain
and make me strong again,
so I in turn can help others feel whole
and loved.

So I learned to listen to my mind,
and speak with them in their state of bliss,
so not a word is ever missed.
And now it's easier than you'd think,
I find.

You too can find the answers that you need
by listening to the words you hear
within your head, not in your ear,
by trusting that your guides
will plant the seed.

Side By Side

I can see you as you sit by the bed, holding your child's hand as they slip in and out of consciousness. You want so much for them to wake up and be well, and indeed we want that too, but the choice belongs to them – it always has.

Why are some children born with ailments or develop them so young? It's a difficult question often pondered by so many, especially when they are going through that experience. It is very hard to explain in a way that would sound acceptable to your human understanding; but these things happen at all ages. The pain of seeing your child very ill is the scariest feeling. But you can cope – indeed, you are more resilient than you give yourself credit for.

Your doctors on Earth are excellent and work tirelessly to expand their knowledge of the physical body and of the mind, but they generally know little about the spirit. That is our job. We are here to shore you up and strengthen you to deal with the greatest of pain, even when you do not feel that you can get through it. Everyone is someone's child and it is this parental aspect that is so challenging every day of your life. Of course, the child will not understand this until they have become a parent themselves, how could they? There is nothing like experience to concentrate the mind and help one learn the lesson more deeply.

You should also understand that you are our children, whom we nurture and protect as much as we can within your chosen path. There are limits to what we can do, but we can also do even more than we already do if you would only ask, only believe in us and in the power of the Light, which is our great parent. It is watching over us and over you, all-knowing, all-seeing and never judging. It helps us create the realities of our worlds even though we may not realise it. But He sees everything and we do not.

Trust, faith, belief – these are words that require all of us to know the possibility that there is more. More for you and yours; more within you than you give yourself credit for.

But right now, all you want is for the hand you are holding to squeeze yours, and for them to know that you are there. Believe me, they do know. And we look after you in the same way that you look after yours. You may feel helpless right now and entirely reliant on human knowledge; but be just as confident that in the unseen world we are assisting you and your child too. Send us your love and ask more people to send their love, for we can work with that and transmute it into something quite beautiful that will bring great ease.

We have used the example of a child, but be assured that it is the same for everyone; no-one is ever left alone when they are unwell in your world. There are always unseen hands supporting everyone involved. Remember the power of prayer, for truly it can change so much. Every word is heard. Every request is processed. No-one gets left out. And when it is time to pass on to our world, you are welcomed as if you are the most important soul; we know your value even if you do not. So please learn this and be valuable to yourself and to your loved ones. Feel the power of love in your lives. And try to live in the now, with the laughter, the pain and the sorrow, for each of these has a part to play in your life.

We send our love and support to all children of every age, so they know they have a friend standing shoulder to shoulder with them. Right now, no matter where you are and whether you are happy or not, we are always there with you. Close your eyes, whisper your prayers and wishes, and we will fold our arms of love around you to let you know that we are listening.

Do Not Fear Death

Do not fear death. It is a fleeting part of life, just another step on the journey of you. There really is nothing to be afraid of; you have chosen the point of your birth and of your death and everything inbetween. Each person has their very own vibration, tune and dance which your soul knows very well. You are never in the wrong place; you may not agree, but that is a fact. When you know this, there is liberation in these words. You are always supported by the unseen people who work with you in the spirit world and you are never, ever alone.

Open your eyes to the amazing possibility of you. Start believing you are beautiful, strong and worthwhile. Do not let any situation hold you back; just let it pass you by with a smile because another will come to replace it just as quickly. Movement is necessary and it is found within the stillness.

Within each of you is a spiritual connection, a direct line to planes of love. How do you access it? Well, stop trying for a start. The secret is to allow it. Let what is to be come around you even if it causes you to be uncomfortable because, when that passes and the stillness returns, it will be all the more special.

So understand you are not forgotten. Know that your thoughts connect to the unseen world daily. Recognise that and make them strong and positive – leave negativity at the door. Take off that heavy coat of worry and strain that you have been carrying for so long and be free. To make a change, you have to make a decision to make a change – one small step on the path can bring amazing opportunities. You changed the path and the smile on your face makes it all worthwhile.

What is your intention? Find it. Just remember to look within yourself each day, for that is where the magic is held. Let a little out. Be brave, the journey is so worth it.

The Way Out

I was sorely stuck in a big black hole,
I don't know how...

But when I peeped inside to check,
what I saw made my cry
for the pains I had were etched upon the veil.

Others had wanted to me to follow them,
and I'd done so out of fear
of being left alone.

But then I read some words that
told me how to
live in this place, this Earth, this now.

And so I left the dark place within
where all my demons live
and came out from behind the rock.

I shook my head clear
and started being me,
no matter that I'm not following any more.

And I felt the strength inside
to free myself of all the chains I'd placed upon my soul
and knew that
I no longer needed to fight.

Soul Growth

Have you watched someone die? Have you watched someone suffer with illness in the body or mind until they leave? Many of you have at some point in your lives and most of you think that they have gone to somewhere better; some call it Heaven and indeed if that is what you want to call it, that's fine by us. There are many names for this place and everyone is welcome in it, no matter what religion or faith they belong to or not.

We find it strange that death seems to be such a taboo as death is just a part of the life that you live on this planet. There should be no fear. What is it precisely that you are scared of? Believe me, there should be no fear as there is only beauty, only love here; this is a place that is always open to you, an amazing place where everyone becomes who they really are, complete, whole and full of life.

We really do not leave at all. We can be with you in the blink of an eye, walking amongst you all the time, taking note of what you do. How come you never notice us? How come you never believe that we are with you? It is because you still rely too much on your physical senses when you should be using your hearts; the love that resides there is the force that links to us, it is your hearts that hold the key to feeling us. It is not by accident that words like 'heartfelt' and 'affairs of the heart' are used in situations relating to love on your plane of life, and you love to be 'in love' when your hearts melt with others'. That is the feeling we have every time we see you, every time we are in your company!

There is place where we come very close to you, a place that is inbetween both planes that you rarely remember when you experience it, and this is in your dreams. Dreaming is a linking of both worlds, a place freely available to all where you are more likely to accept guidance without resistance, where anything can happen and miracles can be created. I am here to tell you that this is not just in the night times but in daylight hours as well; your imagination can bring some beautiful images and thoughts with which you can create miracles. These images manifest in your imagination and can turn into reality if you so wish it. You are much stronger than you think or even know and you can tap into a limitless energy that is there for the taking.

Most of you are not really interested. All you do is struggle on the Earth plane and one has to ask why you do so when there is an alternative? If you need answers, ask. If you need results, ask. If you need to move forward in your life, ask for help to do it. It is in your hands. We are connected, we are family. There are many of you who have had dreams of family members while sleeping or in meditation and who would state that it was "very real". I am here to tell you that it was. How does it make you feel, to know that they are so close? You just have to open your mind to the possibility that there may be something more than you think you know.

There is no need for complications. It is very easy. We love you regardless. Your family who have gone before watch over you, they hear your words of love for them and your pleas of how you wish they were near. And they are nearer than you think. So from this point on, we ask you to try to understand a little more, to try and develop self-belief so that love for you can grow and you may understand that we have not gone completely. We are right here, right now. What is it you would like to say or ask for? It is a pivotal moment so make it real, make it count; ask for what you need and we will make it happen and show you on the Earth that we are part of it, part of the whole.

You could not understand how many facets there are to the bigger picture so we leave that to the scientists of our two worlds. But a time will come when knowing that we are here will be accepted. There is much denial on Earth for various reasons, but do you not have a choice to be who you want to be and believe what you want to believe? In the fast pace of life this is often forgotten, but we know you are so much more.

We are all spirit. You are with a body and we are without but the same energy empowers us. The same energy shows us the path. It is the human mind that changes our experience and that is where choice and denial comes in. As a result of conditioning, some people see us as scary – but we are just the same as you, really we are! It's just that we can now see the truth, whereas while on Earth you only see illusion.

We love you and are proud of you, every one of you. Each one has a soul to grow. This is the only part of you that matters and your choices decide how that soul will grow and at what speed. It is entirely up to you and it can be somewhat daunting to know that we are totally responsible for our actions. But remember that you are not alone on your path.

Close your eyes and what do you feel? You should feel a feather touch on your face, a gentle breeze, an unmistakeable feeling of love. Take that feeling and multiply it in your heart, send it out and it will come back to you threefold. It will bring miracles to you. Be positive. Love yourselves, with all your imperfections for I am here to tell you that to us you are perfect just as you are. Smile and know that you are loved and you will never be alone on the journey.

SPIRIT
GUIDANCE

Through the Window

I study you closely. Your face is nothing short of beautiful. Etched lines of experience stray from your eyes, your skin is smooth, weathered and bronzed. Your hair is long and shiny, tied back, and there is a coloured circle, a wheel, in your hair with a feather hanging down. Your mouth is serious but I am sure I can see the corners start to rise. What are you thinking to cause that semblance of a smile? You are a mystery.

We are seated opposite each other on a rug, rough but very colourful, most of it red; I can hear water and feel the outside breeze but I have no knowledge of where we are and indeed I do not care. This moment is precious, I know, but I do not know why. I say nothing but my thoughts are plenty and swim around my head, wanting to talk; but know I must keep my counsel. I sit and watch.

Around your neck I notice a bone necklace and you smile. It's like you can hear my thoughts, hear my questions, and I realise I can hide nothing from you for we are connected. As I try to absorb all the details of this time, I wish you would speak to me. I wish I could ask questions. Normally I would be getting very frustrated as I would want to ask so much, but I am silent and wait for you to speak. I know you will when you are ready – you are strong and powerful and you give that to me. We never need many words for our connection.

I know we are connected … but how? And then you answer.

"We are connected by love, by a single thought which is all that is needed. The Great Spirit ensures that we have all we need in this life and the next. You ask so many questions that do not need to be asked. You spend so much time thinking and talking – you talk too much and spend very little time accepting the gifts that you have and the path you need to tread.

"Yes, we are connected and have been in many times. I know you well and you always have the same problem – you do not listen. I am not talking about with your ears but with your senses, your heart – leave your mind out of this, it has no part this time. So what is it that links us? What is the connection? It is love. It is only this that matters – love of you, love of me, love of kinship, respect, honour, trust. To give to another with love, to make you happy, to make them happy – what is better than that?

"Why do words have to be complicated, when sometimes it can take so few to let your heart soar – such as 'I need you' or 'I love you'. Are these not beautiful words with great power within them to transform your life? What is more powerful than being who you are and who you need to be – even though you may not know what that is yet?

"So close your eyes and feel Wakan Tanka, feel the love that comes from the Source. It is there however you wish to receive it. We are part of the same soul group and that is why you know me so well. It is only your physical body that need a reply; we do not need words to talk, we only need to feel. We have done this many times and will continue to do so. Do not be scared, I walk by your side and keep you safe. I am a warrior. I loved the plains, I loved the winds that carried all the words I needed. I have learned, as will you."

I sit transfixed listening to your voice, slow and deliberate, meaningful and resonant of something so long ago my mind can't grasp it. You move your hair and touch the wheel.

"The colour red in this medicine wheel is important, it means fire, the sun, the beautiful rays that warm you and the ground, bringing forward new life. I have said I love the winds but the winds from the south are warm and they will strengthen you. I wish you red."

With this you take my hand and stand, you feel real and solid and you smile at me like you'll love me forever. My heart lifts and then sinks as my awareness moves forward and my consciousness returns back to the Earthly moment. I am still seated in the chair staring out of the window. The same view that took me to you, returns me to Earth. The door is open into the garden. I notice how strong the red flowers are blooming today in the corner of the garden. I feel you with me, supporting and loving me. With you by my side I almost feel I could conquer anything. I say a silent 'Thank you'. I see your face in my mind's eye and I close my eyes to draw in a deep breath and steady myself. Suddenly a warm breeze gently blows onto my face and I feel a tear form in my eye.

I smile. No words are needed, I know you are there.

Live

What's your view of Heaven?
Let it go; it's not the way you think it is –
you cannot know.

The love you need is right here,
so stop looking in Heaven for me
for I'm close enough for you to touch.

I could not entice you
or your soul to leave the Earth
nor charm you back, so be content.

With this life you live
you learn and grow;
you will develop all your energies
and the love that you can give.

Here and now,
all is as it should be;
so live your life and know that
I love you.

Pain and Suffering

There is so much pain and suffering in your world that affects the body, mind and spirit and your will. To act or not to act? To love or to hate? To give or to receive? All of you at some point will experience this, but I have come to tell you about something that can help you – something that is free, available to all and that can have a great effect on your lives. Within each of you is an energy that links to the Source. There is no more complicated description needed than this. It links via your heart and via your own energy field, which is all around your body at all times while you live in your body and for a short time thereafter.

And there is an energy that is sent to assist you; you call it healing. This is a slightly misunderstood word. Indeed, healing is given from one soul to another with the intention to send the love – light energy. This energy will then go to where it is needed within your aura and then into your physical, mental, emotional or spiritual self. It always knows its way. That said, there is always a level of responsibility within the receiver to accept the love, and you would be surprised how many find that difficult. The truth is that it may not 'cure'. Many people think they will feel put back together when they have it, and indeed there are many that are. But there are many factors involved.

To us the most important time for healing is at the end of one's life. You may ask what the point of it is then, when it's all over? That may be so for your Earthly life but the blending of energies can help with one's passing to the spirit world; keeping the physical and mental selves calm and assisting the transition itself, helping the person to see the truth. You will have to take my word for that.

There are many healers on your Earth with amazing love and strength. Just to clarify for you – the healing comes from energy.

I once heard it described as the energy that makes the plants grow and the trees bloom, and that is so true. The energy comes through the healer and into you. Sometimes you may feel heat, sometimes you may feel cold and tingles; sometime you may feel nothing and some people feel nervous. There is no need to be, for it's all about love. There are healers who incorporate psychic surgery too. There is no need to berate these people; they know the risks they take in claiming to do what they do. But we want you to know that we support them completely. They all have teams on the side of spirit that work with them for your benefit.

You need to know that no matter who you are the love is there for all of you, the energy is there for all of you. It cannot run out – in fact, there is so much that we want you to use more of it as the more you use the stronger you will become. I don't mean physically but mentally. You will be able to take all that comes your way, one thing at a time.

The forwards steps you have made in science have not yet even scratched the surface of the possibilities that are available for your world. But we do know that healing is starting to be used in your hospitals and that doctors have seen benefits of it. The healing power of love and light is your medicine and it was there before your doctors and your modern medicines and it will be there afterwards. We know that if people only opened their minds just a little, and allowed healing on themselves all the time and not just when they were sick, they would see great benefits. The capacity for pain relief, to calm minds for the confused and even to heal the most serious of diseases, is there. But also know this: if it is your time to pass, then you will, and no amount of healing will stop it. Sometimes one's lifestyle make one ill – what one does, the vices one has. No-one is judging that, but the body is a machine and they don't all work the same way due to the energy around you. What you bring around you affects your energy; so be positive, it makes all the difference.

The human mind has the most amazing capacity, the breadth of which has not even been touched on in your world. The power of the thought process can create miracles in your life. Healing can also be sent over great distances. When there is great tragedy, there is always a great outpouring of grief; you are programmed like this, as this love helps all the sick and departed. People are spurred into action and the need to love one another is great. If you could only apply that all the time, what a different world you would live in!

Everyone is responsible for all their actions. So how do you want to be perceived? If you all made that small change and sent out your healing thoughts daily, they would rise up to join all the others in 'a rope of hope' that would be sent around the world to wherever it was needed. It costs you nothing at all, just a moment of life to give to so many. You are all able to do this if you wish to. That's the key – do you want to give to a stranger, no matter what their lives are like? They may seem to have more than you, be better than you, but do they really? How can you know someone unless you have walked in their shoes? So don't be too quick to make judgements and remember this when you join in with someone who is being unkind to another, as what you give out you will also receive back.

One of the greatest gifts that you have in your lives is hope. You always have it and you always will, there in the lightest of moments and the darkest places. It will shine through all the barriers that you put up and there is no substance on Earth that it cannot penetrate. So send love to the leaders of your world, to be guided by their hearts instead of their minds; send it to the individual on the street and across the world and to your family. Trust your instincts and stand up and be counted, for the power is within each individual and all are as strong as each other. That joint power can create miracles. Do not be afraid for we are watching and encouraging you to move forward with the love and the healing that abounds.

So are you prepared to try? Are you prepared to see what it is like? You can find healers everywhere in your churches. There are healing organisations and indeed many of our communication channels are healers, as mediums know the energy involved already. It is a much higher vibration where this is found. Search it out, find the energy for yourself and believe in yourself. It is your choice to be who you are and no-one has the right to dictate what you do; so be an individual and part of the cosmic love. We are there waiting.

The Door is Open

Did you know that you are never blocked from what you need – not by us anyway? You do tend to do this to yourselves though, and we try to tell you, but you do not listen! When you were children the inner voice seemed so clear; but as you grow more connected to your Earth the voice grows dim – unless you choose to listen all your life. To do this you have to understand that we exist. Many of you do not, or decide that we are not there because that is easier than coping with something that may test your beliefs and stretch your understanding. Tell me, what is wrong with that? You all need a challenge in your lives, or what would be the point? You have to grow your soul.

Imagine your life is a beautiful garden and the people in it are as transient as nature. You have a big old tree that grows at your back, protecting and watching over you, which stretches its roots deep into the earth and grows high into the sky. This is your spirit, strong and beautiful, connected to the physical and the spirit worlds. Then there will be other trees where the roots support one another and hold the ground fast beneath, and flowers that grow in seasons, some lasting for many and some only for a few. The time they need to be with you is all that is needed; don't try and stop this happening as it is already written. You are the main character in the story and what a beautiful story it is. It is the story of you and the possibilities are endless.

So what flowers do you like in your garden? The choice is all down to you. If you don't want weeds you don't have to have them; but don't you find amazing health-giving properties in some of these unconsidered plants? Remember, appearances are not everything. They may be some of the smallest of the plant kingdom, but may also be very powerful in making or breaking a situation. There is always a responsibility that comes with choice, so please be careful what you ask for. If it doesn't work out, that can be scary and put you off trying something new. But we are listening, we are watching and we can help to some degree, so just ask. It may well be the time for your garden to bloom and for you to see miracles.

Enjoy your secret garden of the soul as it is always there, full of colour and delight; give it the credence and the assistance it requires and it will bloom all your life. There will always be enough love, strength and purpose to sustain you. For those who have not found the garden yet, because the door is closed, all you have to do is to want it, to have the intention, and then the key will automatically turn in that door and reveal the magic that is you. Feel yourself in all your strength. See yourself in all your colours and reflect that into your life.

Maybe it is time now. Maybe you have acknowledged who you are? We are waiting on the other side of the door to welcome you. Our arms will wrap around you and we will never let you go, for once you have found it your life will grow like the garden in amazing beauty. Yes, sometimes the rain will fall but this will sustain you, refresh you, and although you may get damp you can always find shelter! So wait for the rain to subside then shake yourself off and be on your way. The garden always needs tending.

A Conversation

From me:

I nearly missed the sign you sent this morning as I drove to work; it was subtle but clear and very gratefully received. I remembered the previous day having the thoughts that caused it – the doubts and fears. Fear of the physicality of life, my job, my home; for a moment I forgot, for a moment I was very human. Then I heard you say that you are with me for the whole journey. You said this as you took my hand and looked into my eyes. I saw you in my dreams. I don't know if I have known you beyond this life, but it feels like it – it feels like lifetimes, and the love you have for me shocks me sometimes.

I try to live up to your expectations and fail all the time, at least in my own eyes. I sometimes wonder if you will suddenly realise that I am just not worth the bother, but in my heart I know you will never leave, as you are the one constant I have and have always had. We have been through everything together and I know we always will.

Thank you for loving me, believing in me, and holding me close as I stumble through this game of life. I will try to do less and get out of the way so you can do more, create more miracles, so I can also do more in this world. Then maybe we can fix it all together.

From you:

There is no separation between us and there never has been. I am not always present 'every day in every way' but my essence is always with you. When times are tough, my hand is in your hand, walking side by side. It was always my choice to be with you and your choice to be with me. There is nothing contrived about this partnership, we are just two parts of the whole. There are many others who act alongside me. Your challenges in this world do indeed belong to you, and you do have to go through them I'm afraid, there is no escape from that – but not alone, never alone.

It irritates me rather that you do not know your own worth! Mmm, we are not perfect either you know, but you give so much to so many and yet you do not see that. Your focus is only to serve and I know the Divine adores you for it; but He also wants you to value yourself.

It is good you understand that you need to stop interfering, to step back and let us help you. Don't worry, all will be exactly as it needs to be. Yes, you may sometimes feel like someone has just thrown you into an abyss and you are falling, but all the while you are being cradled in my love. I have promised this to you and I will never break that bond. Feel me, hold me in your mind, love me with you heart and have faith that I will never let you down.

You are just in transit. I promise the destination will be worth it.

Love and Acceptance

How many times is that today you have felt others' pain? Our capacity to give love is amazing and it is amazing that we do so in circumstances that cause our lives to suffer, where we allow people to possess us in mind or in body. We give away our strength and our power to protect those around us, those closest whom we love. There is nothing we would not do, even put our own lives in mortal danger to protect them. Yet think what value your life has; if you were not here, who would miss you? What we don't realise in the midst of terror is that there are always people who care, who love us, both seen and unseen.

I know that is hard to hear for I was deaf too. I have been in a situation where someone believes they own you, body and soul, to do as they wish with you and not in a good way. I have experienced the desolation and fear that comes with that, when you are scared even to breathe in case you do it the incorrect way that will lead to more pain and fear. It takes superhuman strength to fight it and we have to have a reason to do so, whether it's for one's children, family, the elderly or friends. With me, it was my child; I would have died to protect my child. What is your focus? What is your reason?

Whatever the circumstances you find yourself in, there is always a way out. No-one ever said it was easy, no-one told you that life was going to be like this, but some of us do go through it. It may not start like that; things may seem beautiful and then 'ugly' steps in. In time, part of you starts to believe you should experience this because it's what you deserve, and you become part of that 'ugly' too. Oh, lovely people, that is just not true. You do have the power to walk away. You may be afraid, but you can take back ownership of your life. Just open up to someone, reach for help in the dark and someone will always grab your hand and place you in that life raft to gentler seas. They will wipe your tears and remind you of who you are. Maybe then you can take the action you need to take, find the strength, just maybe…

It is true that not everyone does. It is true that not everyone can. Sometimes, so much shame is felt that eventually you feel nothing, you're empty and bereft. But hold tight to what inspires you, search deep within yourself and find the spark that will ignite your fire. Then move forward, even with trepidation – at least fear causes you to feel something. If you feel fear it means you are alive. If you are alive then you are meant to be here. If you are meant to be here then there is more for you, there always is. Talk to spirit, they will always sustain your humanity. It is at times like this that they surround you and support you. You look but you can't see them; yet listen to your soul, close your eyes and breathe. The wings of angels can flutter in your heart, bringing that love to you that you so desperately need for you and yours.

I wish you the will to try. I wish you the heart to make you strong and the people to care for you, to show you just how special you are to the spirit world and to the people who love you on Earth. Take back your life. Do not allow anyone to take it from you again. Take the hand of friendship that is offered, not out of fear but out of necessity. The people who can help you are brought to you, but you have to make the first step, that is always the case.

Let go of the conditioning and the brainwashing. What do YOU want to do? Where do you want to be? Then take one step at a time. Walk, hold tight, keep your mind focused and believe in a better future and a better life, the one you deserve and the one that is rightfully yours. Escape the prison of your mind and fly.

The stars are yours for the taking. You can be free.

When you get there, the journey starts to be wonderful and the magic is only just beginning.

Mind Power

Your path has been very difficult for a while now and you just don't know why. Let me advise you, dear ones. You are going through nothing short of rebirth, a complete changing of your life and your values.

But the knowledge that you have gathered from the flow of your life can hold you back. Don't fall for that trick. You can tap into the resources of your human spirit and your inner senses will guide you through the dark times. Your journey may not be easy, your path not always visible to you, and not everyone will agree with or love your choices, but you will instinctively know what is right for you. It is important now for you to follow this instinct, this knowing who you are or want to become. It is all you need and it is strong, so ignore all those who try to sway you from it with their hidden agendas or try to manipulate you for their personal gain.

You may find yourself retreating, going back to basics, studying the past. Trace your path back as this is the wisdom inside you pushing you to do a check. Honour yourself, pay yourself the correct attention and you will not go wrong. Open your eyes and see the opportunities in all situations that surround you; believe all your experience can bring a positive air around you – a clearing and a moving forward. Listen to what is said to you, as advice can arrive from the strangest places at the most unlikely times. Remember to behave in a manner that reflects your soul.

The proper use of your wisdom will happen when you live with the flow of your authenticity, being who you are. No sorrow, no regrets. All of these facets make you just perfect. Embrace all the feelings and the experiences. I know that some will be very difficult but they are yours. Look at it like this: within every river there are many bends, so it may meander where it needs.

Each bend in the river is an adventure and with each lesson learned you will grow stronger and better than before. This knowledge will make your wisdom authentic and real. At that point you will then be able to apply those truths to your life's path, bringing to you all that you need.

And no, don't settle for second best, don't just ask "Is this all there is?" Of course it isn't. Use the power of your mind, use the knowledge, use the wisdom and you will be amazing.

Light the Candle

Light the candle, see the way
flooding out upon the ground.
Step from shadow into light
and feel life spreading all around.

With a tiny glow
that special spark within will start
to grow and flame until
it fills your heart.

It becomes more every day
until you can't see it for
it's just become a part of you
and you are so much more.

There will be times when you despair,
lose faith, lose sight, can't hear.
"How am I meant to carry on?
Does no-one see my tears?"

But I am always with you
and my love for you is strong;
if you could just believe in me,
I'll help your path along.

No, I can't tell you what to do –
you make your choices here.
But I am by your side and I
can take away your fear.

Happiness is a State of Mind

I have been watching you for a while, giving away all that you are in the pursuit of others' happiness around you. And this somehow replaces your own happiness. You feel you can't have it yourself, so you throw yourself into the lives of others to 'fix' them. That's very noble but also very irresponsible. Your loyalty should be to yourself first, to make sure that you can provide yourself with the happiness that you deserve – as much as you can in the conditions that you create. You are no victim and no-one can tell you what path to take in your life.

Look back at your memories – how do they make you feel? Memories are just fleeting pieces of time that hold unique pieces of information so we may recall them when needed, to remind us how something should or should not be. They are to be used and acknowledged, and then new ones made to complement the old. They are there to inspire us and make us feel warm and loved; but just as important are the memories that cause us pain, as they teach us to keep away as much as we can from those situations. Upbeat and positive is always preferable though; indeed we are able to create miracles with that particular energy, so try to enhance it a little every day.

Happiness can be fleeting and yet it can also last a lifetime. It may be interspersed with sadness and anger, but that will be short-lived with the right attitude. We can choose not to accept any of the rubbish that arrives in our energy field from other people around us. So remember to protect yourself from those draining energies; draw in a band of beautiful white light around you, and let us do the work for you.

When you feel the love in your heart then all is going very well. You will be happy. You may be one of the lucky ones who feel the love every day. But some people have one difficulty after another. You can always minimise the damage then and move the goalposts. All you have to do is ask for help. You can. You have the power, you are the light. Everyone's experience is different – we are all meant to be different – but life is a matter of perspective.

We want you to be happy, to feel loved and cared for. We create miracles every day in your lives – at least, for those who ask us! We love you.

You Belong to You

In this life, it is important to understand that your mind belongs to you. You can master it and not be mastered by it. There are places that your mind can take you to where a great peace and knowledge can be found. All you have to do is stop for a few minutes, to give yourself a chance to search for a place that suits you.

So you need a few uninterrupted minutes where you can close your eyes and sink into a different reality, a place where you can see the people who have passed before you and where you can talk with them as if they were with you now. This is entirely possible. You just have to try to find that peace – a rare thing in your world, but achievable if you try. When you decide to do this for the first time, it may be that too many thoughts will interrupt. Don't try to stop them – allow them to come in, acknowledge them then let them vanish. Imagine they are on a conveyor belt, see them and let them go.

Wherever you find yourself when you meditate, just go with it. It may be a beach, a forest, on water or just an ordinary place. Go anyway, it's all part of the journey so don't question it. When you give yourself these moments regularly you will notice a change within yourself and in others around you, subtle and gentle yet the effects can be huge. It can bring great change. Everyone has the ability to go into this peace and be quiet. Everyone can feel the love that comes with these experiences; maybe not every time, but if you persevere you can gain great knowledge because you are altering the state you're in, you are choosing something more. It is so important that you know about this. It's not difficult, you just have to commit to yourself now. How hard can that be?

This feel-good state is free to access and can give you great insight into problems that you may be experiencing. You may not always understand it at the time, but make a note of the experience in a journal and over time you will see a pattern or a message being made clear to you. That said, sometimes stubbornness can stop you from moving forward. You do not always know what is right for yourself! But if you listen, you will be led down the path that is correct for you. There will always be challenges, but every time you connect to the silence you will be given tips and tools to help you overcome them.

Silence can be deafening. It's hard to hear and just go with it, but don't give up. Try it, you may find just what you are looking for to make everything fit. Never give up, as we never give up on you, and over time you will find that you will not be a slave to your mind any longer. You will realise that you are indeed the master and have been all along.

Time Consciousness

If you could turn back the hands of time, what exactly would you change? Would you be sorry for some of things you have said or done or even achieved at the expense of others? Would you wish your loved ones to be around, those who have left you, those in spirit and on the Earth? Would you be in a better position than you are now? How do you know this would be the case? That's the trouble – you don't. You actually know very little before it happens.

We have all on occasions regretted some of the situations that have occurred in our lives, but they are done and we cannot take them back. We can, however, repair things a little. We have a chance to fix them here and now. The more we try now, the more the universe supports us. All we have to do is believe and have the intention to heal things. We are all capable of miracles.

I want to tell you something mind-blowing. You are living more than one existence at one time and in each place you are the same, yet different, living different lives and gaining as much experience as you can to let your soul grow. There are times when all the pieces of you come together, but not often and when they do your consciousness expands.

When you sleep, your consciousness does not; it travels. It's only your body that needs the physical rest. There have been many descriptions of this and it's hard to define it in a human way; there are many trying to prove it. Consciousness means that you perceive thoughts and feelings, which then cause your body to act in certain ways. But there are many levels of consciousness. When all your human vibrations are raised and eventually you work side by side with us daily, you will know about this and all will become clear, though that is some time away yet.

That said, your conscious mind is much stronger than you can imagine. It has the capacity to affect physical life on many levels. What you think and what you believe, you can achieve. Intention is one of the most powerful thoughts in this universe and it all comes from your conscious mind. So ask yourself – what is your intention, what do you want to achieve? All is possible.

If you allow your thoughts to be affected by others, then you allow them to influence your life and that should not be. It is your choice and your responsibility always to care for yourself as you care for others, for you are important to the plan. Some are even trying to manipulate consciousness for ill motives. But it can never be harnessed; each of us is an individual, each of us is imperfect, so no two will ever have the same mind. We have choice and free will, so there is always something that will get in the way.

You should embrace all that you are. If you have had situations in your life where you could have handled things better and you know it – well, you made the choice. It's difficult accepting that we are wrong and sometimes we really are! But no matter what you do, we don't wish to alter you in any way. Equally, you may be right and someone else is wrong and it is just as frustrating for you when you cannot change this. All becomes clear when a soul reaches the world of spirit; everything is known and one's whole life experience fits into place, bringing lightness of being.

So always just try to improve yourself and others whom you can affect. Those who do not want to listen, do not make them part of your personal goal but let them go their own way as they will have to learn for themselves. There are only certain people who will actually listen, and it will be clear to you at the times what is needed. There will be no need to search. Words will be passed to you at the correct time in life by the correct people and they will make all the difference. This is as it should be. Meanwhile, never believe that you know someone else's life better than they do, because you cannot – their path will not be the same as yours.

The spirit world offers you the gift of 'worry no longer'. The realities of Earth are that we attend the classes that have been set for us and achieve as much as we can in our lifetime. We chose it so we live it, laugh and cry through it, and it belongs to us whether we deem it to be right or wrong. So hold your head up and look forward, for it's the future where the excitement lies and there are no more regrets. We look forward to meeting you later and seeing your face when the recognition strikes and you are free. Until then we watch over you every day. We can assist your dreams wherever they may take you. The possibilities are endless.

Today

Today's a gift, a chance to grow and lose concern
for all the past, for all that's gone.
Each new day comes before the dawn
so let it bring you what you need, the lessons
that can make you strong and help you grow.
Within the present is the gift
for you alone, so never wish your days to be done
but take each day with grace
for what you need is here and now.
And if events upset your plans,
don't feel displaced, remember that
it's all about the striving not the reaching
and you will achieve your heart's desire,
don't doubt it.
We've told you once and we shall again,
your path is right
and if you look beyond what you can see
you'll know we're waiting, listening out
and we can help you now.
So open up the gate, step through
without a thought of looking back,
and you'll find inner strength
and none can doubt your will today.
And when you feel you can't move on,
exhausted by today,
you must remember there's a plan
where we're all joined to manifest reality;
you only must believe
and all solutions that you need are given free.
We are together, part of you within your soul,
to help you live your life today.

Leap of Faith

I am at the end of my rope! This is the end of the road! Time to give up now... We hear this every day. Each of you will go through something akin to despair and feel so shaken that you believe there is no escape, no way out of the quagmire you believe is your life.

I am here to tell you that this is not the case. This is not the way we want you to act; and you also know deep within you that this is not the way you want to be either. These most difficult of times are when we are with you, very close, almost like a second skin. And it is at these times when you spiritually leap forward in your lives, in your souls' growth, and find out the real measure of you.

Perhaps you are standing on a cliff edge and as you look below you can't see what is there and it frightens you. Somewhere in your psyche you have belief, but there are times when you do not feel it. So can you step off into that abyss? Are you scared? Of course you are. But are you alone on that edge? No, of course you are not for we are all around. We have put your wings on your back; and there is no doubt that the moment you step off the edge you will fly on the wings of change and opportunity, strengthened by our love. It is a matter of faith.

Opportunity is not always packaged in the way we think it should be. It is not always tied with a big ribbon, but sometimes in nondescript brown paper and we just have to accept it for what it is. Maybe you do not want to do that, but no-one said life was going to be easy. It is a fact if that you really want something to occur, it is totally achievable. Your mind has the capacity to bring you all you need and want; but if you do not want to put the effort into getting it, then it will not happen because you could not have wanted it that much in the beginning. It's simple. This is your life, your experiences and your choices, and if they agree with others' it is only because you have chosen so.

Then again, you may make a change and find that it just flows; then you will wish you had done it before and will wonder what it was you were afraid of in the first place. Well, you won't know until you try it, will you?

So what is this faith and where is it found? Everyone can choose what to put their faith in, so start with yourself. Faith in yourself will never let you down because you are just as you are meant to be any time. Use your skills to build your faith in whatever and whomever you choose. Not all of these will work out for you – you will be let down by others and you may let them down too – but we all make mistakes; it is a question of balance that must be maintained. It is the spiritual law. Fear not, it is all part of the plan.

So as you step off into your future, do you hear the whisper of the wind and feel the wings on your back supporting you as you move forward? Do you feel the warmth of our love? It is there, it is always there. So leap and find your faith.

Where Do You Live?

'Religion is for people who are afraid of going to Hell;
spirituality is for those who have already been there.'

This is very thought-provoking. Most religion does imply that there are two places for you to go to after the passing of your current existence. One is good and one is not so good. And it all depends on how you act out your life. Partly this is true, in that your life and all you do in it is your own responsibility. No-one can force you to do anything you do not want to. However, there being 'two places' is incorrect. There is only one – at least, for the time you choose to be there.

It is a different place, a parallel universe that is full of developing possibilities for you to grow and learn and understand more. This place has many names across many worlds and dimensions; indeed, it is a world in its own right. Whatever you call this place is fine by us – we just call it 'home'. Within it, you will go to wherever you need to be, but rest assured that you will all go there. No-one is excluded; everyone has a soul and a personality, do they not? The universal laws will decide each one's eventual destination.

So where is it that you live, where do you currently call 'home'? Is it filled with beautiful furniture and do you have precious possessions? Are you a person of fame? Or are you someone who owns very little materially and perhaps would like more? The material attributes themselves mean nothing on this side of life, only the way that you obtained them matters. Did you treat people correctly? Did you share kindness? Did you give to others on your life path? Did you even know you were being tested, to see what you would decide, and that the decision to do this was your own? Well, you do now! What are you going to do about it?

Have you judged others? Of course you have, everyone does; opinion and judgement are awfully close, it's just the feelings and thoughts behind them that make the difference. So be careful: what you sow, so shall you reap. That said, not everyone can be charitable all of the time. Sometimes you have to hide away and take care of yourself first. And everyone has strong emotions, responses brought on by the soul, by who we are, and we all respond differently on the physical plane. You will see the results when you come here, how your actions and decisions affected others whether you knew it or not. You will be shown what the point of it all was. You knew there had to be one – it could not be all for nothing.

When you come over to the spirit side of life, it can take a short while to adjust, depending on your circumstances. You forget very quickly the physical possessions. However, your loved ones are an entirely different matter; that bond is forged through love and you cannot escape it even if you want to. The feeling permeates everything you know and are and it will show you the way. There is a lot to learn and to see on this side – we do not call it a world for nothing – and the opportunity to be the real you is most refreshing. Do not fret, you will be supported and helped. Your family and friends will be with you all the way through your journey for as long as you wish, until the point that you decide to do something more.

Who you are now is transitory and you are changing every day, so enjoy the challenges of life. When you come here it will be like coming home.

Who You Are Today

Do you know who you are today? Is it someone you know well? Or are you going through a metamorphosis yet? We cannot always stay in the situations we find ourselves in. We all have to move on and our souls and energies will evolve over time to bring us to a point of massive change. It will happen to all of us at some point. So is yours near?

When it happens, the best advice would be to hold on tight and to know that it is meant to be. It is a rollercoaster and the ride can be very fast. It is in these times that we doubt ourselves. Situations we are experiencing may not be of our own making but we are still meant to live through it; so we must use our strength, wherever we find it, and use it to manifest our change. It will happen whether we fight it or go with it. You may ask "Why me?" Well, why not? It is just meant to be, part of the soul's journey along with that of others who interact with us. Everyone is connected. Some of these others we may judge and dislike, but we all have to see both sides of the coin. People will test us and push us, but then how do we know light until we have had the dark? We all know right from wrong in our hearts, it is intrinsic to who we are.

We wish you all love and strength and may the words you read here inspire you on your path. If you can share your own thoughts with others, be brave and share the troubles, it may be a little easier. Remember, the destination is written but the journey is not and we do all have choices along the way. The problem is figuring out which ones are good for you and which are not. If you share your life and thoughts with spirit and with the people close to you, you will be moved to act in the correct ways. Don't hide yourself away. The problem is that if you climb into a big black hole, the sides are smooth and steep and getting yourself out will be very difficult. On the other hand, there is a way out at any time – you just have to believe that you can do it.

Believe in spirit. We love you and care for you and we hope that in these words you find the promise to move forward. Believe in yourself even if no-one else seems to – that is the first step to perfection. It will not be reached in a hurry, there will be many steps and many lifetimes, so that should give you hope because you get more than one chance to succeed. The choice is yours, it always shall be yours.

Feel our wings around you, feel our love by your side, and watch out for the angels in your daily life – the ones without wings – for they are there to bring you hope and to make you smile. You are loved so give love, as love is all.

Belief

Are the eyes that flame with love human?
Is the love that burns, yours for the taking?
Yes.
Open your heart and feel the arms wrap around you,
keeping you safe from pain,
loving you, urging your soul to soar.
Close your eyes
and feel me...

True Purpose

When the true purpose of what is happening is hidden from your view and your frustration is causing you fear – hang on in there. It may not make any sense now, but one day it will. A blessing is on its way to you. It will bring great change and purpose to your life and once that happens many more blessings will follow. So hold tight and feel the love around you.

That Feeling

Close your eyes.
Feel my breath on your cheek
and my hand on your shoulder.
I am very close.
Can you hear my voice?
Listen, I am here,
don't ever doubt me.
Our hearts are one,
beating together like a drum
that's part of you and part of me.
You fill my soul with your lilting voice.
Let me fill your heart with my love.
Let me ease your journey.
Let me love you, adore you.
I am not of your world,
but ask for me to appear in your life
and I will.
I am ready for the adventure.
Are you?

Seasons

As the seasons of your soul turn, so your life grows into something amazing. Perhaps you do not see the powerful forces in your life moulding you to the tree that supports you, the roots that ground you and the branches reaching upward, searching for so much more than you have now, for the possibility of greater opportunity. It is true that many do not see the wood for the trees. When your miracle is close, it would be easy to miss it if you have your head in the clouds – come back down to Earth!

Feel the reality of life and embrace it, no matter what it is, for you have no idea where it is leading. Feel your dreams and embrace them as they join as one in your soul. Allow the feelings to permeate your energy and your consciousness; feed them with your thoughts, the food that sustains the magic.

Sometimes it may feel as if you are falling into an abyss, but fear not for you are not alone. How can you fall when we have wings to sustain you? It really is not complicated. We react to your thoughts and help you to manifest them; but you have to do your part too. We are all part of the One so you have the ability to tap into our power the moment you start to believe it – so that's what you have to do. Get rid of all expectations in your mind, focus on your goal and allow the miracle to come to you. Speak your truth and be who you need to be for now. Tomorrow will take care of itself, no matter what the season of your life.

Believe in us, in yourself, and in the divine power that incorporates all.

Fear

What are you afraid of? Has someone hurt you, stolen part of you away? Why did you let them? Of course you will say that you did not allow it to happen – but you did. Every one of us on the Earth gives and takes, whether it is through kindness or unkindness, through fear, anger or love.

These are emotions and we all have a choice whether or not to act on these feelings. Yes, it is our choice – why is that so difficult to understand? Of course, that means that we are in control, and that's scary but it's the truth. We all have responsibility for our lives, no matter what happens. Great happiness or great sadness always happens by cause and effect – this is the law of the universe. You may find yourself on a very happy path that turns sour very quickly, or vice versa, but each is caused by a decision or a choice by someone.

So what can we do? "No point then, is there?" so many say. "We have no control if there is this universal law." But of course you have control. You have choice and you can make decisions. You can make the choice to ask us for help and then make the decision to get out of the way, so we are able to help you.

Fear is but a word describing an emotion. But really there is nothing to be afraid of, for all is as it should be. You have already chosen this. Perhaps you will only understand this when you reach this side of life.

We love you, you are very loved by the Divine and you are never alone. Your friends and family who have gone before watch over you and care, do not doubt that. They ask you to consider what is the worst that can happen? Think about it, then realise that nothing really matters; only love and belief.

We want you to live your lives with all the possibilities it can bring. You have to experience all your challenges as only then will you truly appreciate the great love that goes with positivity. You are strong, beautiful and human, so accentuate the positive and go with the flow. Your angels are there to help, and they are listening.

Faith

Dry your tears,
you can let go, you can be free;
you only have to trust in me:
I am your friend, I know your past
and understand your fears
but know they will not last.
The power that others sometimes wield
is strong but don't allow it
to deter you, for the here and now
is only an illusion
created before you came to Earth.
To this we both elected
that our wisdom and our fates would chime,
and you will understand in time
that it's your choice.
You're on the path, you know the way;
and I walk with you,
listening, loving, caring
whether you agree or doubt as problems mount
yet I am sharing them.
Everything is for a reason
and it doesn't matter how long it lasts,
I promise you are not alone
and you'll be stronger when it's passed.
So love me just as I love you
for good or ill, don't shut me out;
I see you beautiful and perfect
and I'll help you understand what life's about.
You're so much more than you yet know,
and if you only trust in me
I'll show you how to let go of your fear.

Spirit Guides

One of the most frequent questions we are asked is, "Do you know who my guides are?" So we want to give you a simple view of this. Everyone who wishes to learn about the spirit world is always so interested in who is leading them. The need to know always amuses – and sometime irritates – us; but I suppose that is just human interest. I understand, some of us were human too!

You all have a name on Earth but it is just a label, it does not define you in any way. What is important – what defines you – is what you do, the way you behave and the love and compassion that you show to others. That is how growth and learning is achieved.

One thing is for sure – the people who work with you always choose to do so and, at some level, you choose to allow them to. They are just ordinary souls who have moved over to the higher planes and they have chosen to work in this way to move forward with their own progression. You know, the spirit world is just like your world. As you are here on Earth, so shall you be in spirit, with a body that can be felt and arms to hold loved ones; and they do hold you – but in their hearts. They may be strangers, they may be loved ones or not even human. But slowly, if you are open enough to want to look a little deeper into life and love and the spirit world around you, then they will be there to assist and they will be very happy about that. However, even if you are not aware of the spirit world, the angels who guide you are always around. Some like to call them 'guardian angels'. They do not mind what you call them, they just hope that you know they are with you.

Guides can be met in dreams, in meditation, or (if you are really lucky) they can manifest on Earth at important times in your life and turn it around. The stranger who just appears at the most propitious time is not there by accident; you may never realise who they are as they look as solid and real as you. They do it because they can, because you are unconditionally loved always. When you feel at your lowest ebb is when they are closest; but that is also when you are so wrapped up in the human condition that you may feel them the least.

You are all on this journey together, they are learning and growing with you, it is a joint, group effort. The soul group to which you belong can change as you do, but there are always some stalwarts who stay with you throughout your life. Your soul group will consist of many from this world and the next and you may be connected over many lifetimes. You are like different facets of a diamond, each shining its light as one. That is why it is very important to understand that you are the light: you belong to that essence, the complete God Light. You are perfect in the now. You are doing exactly what you should and are in the correct place for you. Now, you may dispute this, but you are in this place of illusion to grow, to expand your knowledge; so the secret is to use whatever you can to play your part of the game the best way you can. Perfection can never be reached on Earth though, else what would be the point of anything further? There is always more you can do, more you can achieve and be. All you have to do is to trust the flow of your life.

Look around from this point and see what happens. Ask your guides, angels or protectors to step closer to you. Ask them to reveal their 'calling card', then search for the synchronistic event that shows it to you. Look for life's patterns and look for miracles – they do happen.

So open your heart, the area that all love comes from. This is the key to all you wish to manifest in your life: love really is all you need.

Always do it your own way. So spread as much love as you can, and don't forget the most precious person – yourself – because you are light. Your glow is amazing and beautiful. Open your eyes. Open your heart and see it and believe in us as we do in you, for all your human life and beyond. And one day we shall meet and hold you close and you will understand everything and wonder why you ever struggled in the first place!

God's light is in everything and everywhere, the past and the future, it never wanes even in the darkest depths. You can't escape it even if you try. So escape instead from the confines of your mind and link to the consciousness of the universe. Think for yourself and be free.

> The winds of love blow through your life –
> feel the chill and the change,
> be brave and reach out to us.
> We can make all the difference.

Fear

Fear is not real, it's only there to make you think again;
but it can deceive you,
and exaggerate the pain you feel
unless you let it all just go away.
Send it back to us and let us deal with it
and guide your journey now.

Is it really easy? Yes, it truly is
when you are brave and open up your heart
and let the spirit give you all you need.
We promise to impart the knowledge that you seek
and put your life on track,
to lift you up when you are feeling weak.

Be proud of who you are right now, relax and smile
for we have shaken off the darkness;
and while you're wondering if you do believe
in us, your spirit carers,
we are walking right beside you anyway
and always there.

So talk to us, tell us your pain and anger too –
don't worry, no-one judges you
for God's love comes on angel wings.
It's there whenever there is need.
So let go of your fear, for all you ever need is love,
and it shall make you free.

Prayer

I heard your prayer to me today,
when you were worried, feeling lost …
It made me smile to hear this
for we'd crossed swords of late,
when in your anger you had doubted me,
refused to listen, turned your face away
from the angel right in front of you.

But I am here to help you
even when you crease your brow
or shout and stamp;
I'm here to light the way, to light your soul
and help you onwards,
give you strength when nights are black.

Take my hand, I'll lead you through
all the many things you have to learn.
I know what you need to be free;
so can you try to open up your inner eye to see
the real you and the real me?

I want your loving heart to feel
the love that you are owed for all time,
loved and valued and adored by all
for being you, a star.
So please try to accept it and believe.

So trust in me and talk to me again.
It doesn't matter where or how,
just in your own way, fiery or in peace,
I hear your words and smile for love of you.

And I shall fix and re-arrange the path
to help you learn as you go on,
our hands held tight,
for I shall always guide you.
Feel my love, my faith, my strength,
given that you may overcome your trials.

And when it's over you will see
how much I've loved you and you've loved me;
and we shall laugh together in the light.

Can't!

"There's no such word as can't!" How many times have you been told this as a child? But there's a problem with this for there is such a word and it's one that causes us really big problems when we hear it and use it; then we look for obstacles to put in the way because it's hard to make changes or go against the grain of life. If people all flowed in one direction all the time, then nothing would get discovered or created and the change that you need would not manifest itself.

But we have the choice to accept it or not – it is our mission. It may be difficult and that causes us to doubt ourselves. It may change the course of our life to go down a dark alleyway that we can't see the end of, so we become frightened and stumble around in circles in the dark instead of walking to the end of the alleyway where the light is bright. Why do we not understand that?

Sometimes as we become embroiled in our lives it is true that the troubles can outweigh the pleasures. We allow the negative attitudes of other people (who are in fact going through similar troubles) to affect us. We all suffer in different ways and the trials that are so painful for us may not be so for others. Each has their nemesis that will have to be faced sometime, and it is then that we leap spiritually. Why is this? It is the soul's journey, good or bad as we perceive it to be, that makes us who we are here. It brings people around us who love us – and those who do not. That's fine, as not everyone can gel together. What one feels as painful will not seem the same to another so they will not really understand; we have to walk in someone's shoes to know the lessons within their experiences. These experiences mould our personality, identify our strengths and weaknesses and show us the areas that we need to grow in.

Now here's the rub. It is you who believes in and says the word "can't". We in spirit do not believe in that word. Yes, there may be a delay in getting what you want for you have to figure out how to get it. If you ask us we can help you – but ultimately it is up to you. Sometimes you have to be very brave and speak what is really in your heart.

These words may be difficult to be heard, but if you can no longer continue then change has to happen, no matter what others' opinions are. Only you can make the right decisions for you. We can all live together and be who we are, but then we must learn to accept that all is just as it should be, even though it may not be as we want it to be. The change does not have to be great. Just do something different, that's enough to change the energy around you and then the rest will follow.

In this process of denial, where you frequently find yourself, it is easy to think that you are going through this alone. But you are not. You may not have too many people around you physically for whatever reason, but that does not matter. The spirit world is always around you, loving you and encouraging you, frequently bringing signs of our presence as you carry on your daily existence. We will just fit into every day. Sometimes you will miss us; you will have to look, but then you have to see and also hear. Was that a coincidence or a sign? There is no coincidence for everything has a reason; if you think like this every day then life will seem easier – you can compartmentalise it better within your mind. No-one is against you, apart from if you allow others' feelings, words and actions to penetrate your energy and affect it. You can say "No". But you may need these experiences to push you, to test you so that you may live through them. It may be a rollercoaster but at least you are moving in some direction! Standing still and silent is never an option.

So drop the 't' and use "Can". You can achieve and you are beautiful and you deserve love and fruitful experiences in your life. Your past conditioning by those who raised you has an influence on you, but you have a choice whether to let that influence guide you now and in your future. Only you know if it is and was right for you. Make your own decisions, make your own choices for you. You will be amazed how people will change alongside you – how everything fits in place beautifully. Watch your life improve. So the next time you're about to say "I can't" – stop. Can you really?

This happens already but we say it out of habit and out of fear. Well, you know what they say: feel the fear and do it anyway. Love yourself, hug yourself, because we do feel it and we will all through our physical lives. Don't be worried about judgements – you know in your heart what is right and wrong. The concept of 'what goes around, comes around' is true; and when the time comes for you to pass to spirit you will see yourself for all that you are and everything will make sense. Only you will judge you. Some of us were there on Earth once so we know how you feel. We have walked in your shoes and we have seen the result. And I can tell you: it is all worth it.

Some are leaders and some are followers and that is as it should be. So which are you? Are you content to sit back and allow others to define you? That can happen if you allow it. Or are you going to stop saying "I can't" and take control of your life in a beautiful way, to make you smile every day. The destination is written but the journey is not, not completely. You have free will, so use it, expand it and inspire other people to expand themselves. You are your own inspiration, it is all there within you. All you have to do is to remember that all you need is within you. When you are in darkness, just remember that there is no measure of dark, only of light; and there is always light in the darkest of places. Never give up.

You may want more and if it is to come then it will be. Yet we know that you are beautiful just as you are, in all your imperfection. If you were perfect, you would not be there; we have all trodden similar pathways and none of us have yet reached perfection. Does it exist? Yes it does. It is the light that shines in the darkness when you need it most, the light of love of beauty, the light within me and the light within you that watches over us, that whispers to our souls and always says "I can".

Strength

This morning, I saw you as you climbed out of bed and readied yourself for the day ahead. You did not know I was there, but I was.

You were tired – the week had been difficult for you, the people, the situations. How to overcome the problems of each day?

But what exactly are those problems? Usually they are what you make them, how you perceive them and how you let them affect your life. So do not allow them to – do not complicate the matters of your heart and mind, they are complicated enough just as they are.

Step one foot literally in front of the other and do not try to cope with all the stresses on your own. Share them with me, tell me what you need, then step away and allow me to help you.

Easy does it, little by little, your miracle is possible.

I am still watching you, keeping nearby, so close your eyes, relax and feel my wings around you.

How Rich Are You?

Did you know that some people are so poor in this world that they only have money? For them, the only value they count on in their lives consists of physical accoutrements that are completely superficial. After all, when you leave the Earth you can't take them with you. We all know such people who adore their money and all the trappings of their physical existence, at least for a while. The problem with this is that all these so-called valuables are very easy to lose – by one's own decisions or those of others who impact one's life.

It is no problem to us in spirit that you wish to have the objects and the comforts of life, no problem at all, just as long as you understand that they can vanish as quickly as they arrive. Everything on your plane of existence has an energy, a vibration that emanates right down to the cellular level, and all energies have an effect on yours. If the energy needs to change around you it will; it finds its way because it has to.

The richness of your life does not lie in the physical objects you have, but in all your energy fields. All the emotions that make you who you are – a woman or man, a lover, a giver or a healer, whatever you know yourself to be – and the giving of yourself for the betterment of others, this is where the real richness lies. So be empathic, try to understand why others around you have their problems. Take a few moments longer than you normally would to listen to them, for there may be a very simple way in which you can help the situation; the person involved has not come around you by accident. So try to step up to the mark. You are naturally rich in love, it is engrained in your soul; and if you do not give it, that is your choice – perhaps because you are afraid of how you might be seen in your world. But the world belongs to everyone.

You have the capacity to be rich beyond your wildest dreams, and it won't cost you a penny. For whatever you give, you most certainly do receive. Even if you don't have much, give a little and it will always return to you. There are always people around you who are needy and ready to receive. It really is not a difficult choice. Just do something unexpected. Be the person you were born to be. The richness of your soul and your heart will swell, bringing unexpected magic into your life. Then you will know just how rich you are.

Stuck?

Are you stuck in a position that you want to get out of, but can't? Or at least that's what you believe? The sticky situations that you find yourself in are always by your own design and your own choice! They are your responsibility and you cannot blame anyone else for your misfortunes.

Whether a situation is actually sticky is, however, a matter of perception. It may always have been so but you did not want to see it, and maybe something new has come in your life to cause you to see more clearly. Don't make excuses! Change what needs to be changed, but be sure it is what you want because going back is rarely an option; things never return to the form they once had. First though there may be a battle within yourself as you choose the path you need to take.

Now, to make you feel a little better, there are points in your life that have already been decided before you arrived here. But the journey to those points is not decided, so it's up to everyone to travel that journey well, remembering that you have personal responsibility for everything you do. You may like to blame situations on other people, but in your heart you know they lie at your feet.

So what is it that you would like to change in your life: a relationship, a job, a belief? Or are you just looking for something more? All these require action from you. We cannot make decisions for you as there are other people who will also be affected by those decisions. But when you feel the pull to try something new, or a great attraction to another person and you just don't understand why, sometimes it is wise to listen to these markers.

We all want more – that is ingrained deeply within us. But understanding grows and then we realise that actually we need none of it, that we are perfect just as we are. The physical attributes of this life can make it a little more comfortable, and some of us will achieve these comforts, but what about those who cannot have them through no fault of their own? It may be due to where they were born in the world or due to their nature. Does that make them any less perfect? Of course not – we all have the light within us. Sometimes we can be blind to our own inclination towards greed. But let's not judge, it not our place to do so and the only person who judges you is yourself.

So do not let your mind hold you back for it can be your own worst enemy at times. The good deed, the bad deed, it is all your choice; just try to act for the best of reasons and know that spirit are watching and walking with you always. It is in these difficult times of change that people feel most alone, but let me tell you that it is then that we walk closest to you. Trust you heart. Trust your feelings. They are a more accurate measure of you than what money and status you have. And when we get to the spirit world, we are all equal.

To give from the heart is a wonderful gesture that you will feel acutely, and you will gain so much more in your life this way. You see, there has to be a balance in everything. If you become out of balance, it can affect your physical, emotional and spiritual health. So listen only to love and have people around you who love you.

Yes, we all need a challenge or how else would we move forward in our lives? Staying still is never an option. What you should do is to concentrate on yourself and do the best that you can for others, yet allow other people to be themselves, as they have to grow in their own light and you in yours. That includes children, parents, brothers and sisters – support them but don't make their decisions for them. It can be difficult to watch people close to you go through the stresses and strains of life; but rest easy, they have their helpers too. We are all linked through the same Source.

So feel the love in your life and feel the pain, move forward fearlessly and allow your miracles to change you to be who you really are.

Inner Child

Which part of you is that child? I am here to tell you that it is there at all times, waiting patiently to be released. So what are you afraid of? Let it go and laugh for a few minutes on a regular basis, do something childlike. Be a child, it is who you really are.

We are surprised by how soon many people forget how to be a child, how eager you are to grow into an adult and leave aside childish things. During the first years of life we grow at a greater pace than at any other time. It is a time of discovery and beauty and – should be – of love. So why be in a hurry to leave it? It is true that not all childhoods are happy, but being childlike – playing on a roundabout, laughing with friends – is always good and has a greater effect on us than any other energy. It is very good for healing all negativity. It is a state of mind.

There are many things you once were that you are not now. Is this for the better? Perhaps not. So find a little fun and happiness, let the child escape and be a little naughty. You'll find that you have greater clarity of mind and a better balance in knowing what is important. You may not be able to return to the halcyon days, but you can create new ones and learn to love the laughter once again. This will allow greater possibilities into your life that you never saw previously. Laughter can do this like nothing else can.

You may have to be a little brave and step out of your comfort zone. Try it and watch for the sunshine. It can really change your life.

If you have enjoyed this book

Local Legend is committed to publishing the very best spiritual
writing, both fiction and non-fiction. You might also enjoy:

SIMPLY SPIRITUAL
Jacqui Rogers (ISBN 978-1-907203-75-6)

The 'spookies' started contacting Jacqui when she was a child and
never gave up until, at last, she developed her psychic talents and
became the successful international medium she is now. This is a
powerful and moving account of her difficult life and her triumph
over adversity, with many great stories of her spiritual readings.
The book was a Finalist in The People's Book Prize national
awards.

AURA CHILD
A I Kaymen (ISBN 978-1-907203-71-8)

One of the most astonishing books ever written, telling the true
story of a genuine Indigo child. Genevieve grew up in a normal
London family but from an early age realised that she had very
special spiritual and psychic gifts. She saw the energy fields around
living things, read people's thoughts and even found herself
slipping through time, able to converse with the spirits of those
who had lived in her neighbourhood. This is an uplifting and
inspiring book for what it tells us about the nature of our minds.

THE QUIRKY MEDIUM
Alison Wynne-Ryder (ISBN 978-1-907203-47-3)

Alison is the co-host of the TV show *Rescue Mediums*, in which she puts herself in real danger to free homes of lost and often malicious spirits. Yet she is a most reluctant medium, afraid of ghosts! This is her amazing and often very funny autobiography, taking us 'back stage' of the television production as well as describing how she came to discover the psychic gifts that have brought her an international following.
Winner of the Silver Medal in the national Wishing Shelf Book Awards.

A SINGLE PETAL
Oliver Eade (ISBN 978-1-907203-42-8)

Winner of the national Local Legend Spiritual Writing Competition, this page-turner is a novel of murder, politics and passion set in ancient China. Yet its themes of loyalty, commitment and deep personal love are every bit as relevant for us today as they were in past times. The author is an expert on Chinese culture and history, and his debut adult novel deserves to become a classic.

RAINBOW CHILD
S L Coyne (ISBN 978-1-907203-92-3)

Beautifully written in language that is alternately lyrical and childlike, this is the story of young Rebekah and the people she discovers as her family settles in a new town far from their familiar home. As dark family secrets begin to unravel, her life takes many turns both delightful and terrifying as the story builds to a tragic and breathless climax that just keeps on going. This book shows us how we look at others who are 'different'. Through the eyes of Rebekah, writing equally with passion and humour, we see the truth of human nature…

5P1R1T R3V3L4T10N5
Nigel Peace (ISBN 978-1-907203-14-5)

With descriptions of more than a hundred proven prophetic dreams and many more everyday synchronicities, the author shows us that, without doubt, we can know the future and that everyone can receive genuine spiritual guidance for our lives' challenges. World-renowned biologist Dr Rupert Sheldrake has endorsed this book as "…vivid and fascinating… pioneering research…" and it was national runner-up in The People's Book Prize awards.

These titles are all available as paperbacks and eBooks.
Further details and extracts of these and many
other beautiful books may be seen at

www.local-legend.co.uk

Lightning Source UK Ltd.
Milton Keynes UK
UKOW04f1215220714

235547UK00017B/743/P